TO BE HAPPILY MARRIED

TO BE HAPPILY MARRIED

Mohinder Singh

KALPAZ

ISBN: 978-81-7835-976-2

Price : ₹ 720

First Published 2013

Published by

Kalpaz Publications
C-30, Satyawati Nagar,
Delhi - 110052
E-mail: kalpaz@hotmail.com Ph.: 9212142040

Laser Typesetting : Rajender Vashist, Delhi
Printed at : G. Print Process, Delhi

Cataloging in Publication Data--DK
Courtesy: D.K. Agencies (P) Ltd. <docinfo@dkagencies.com>

Mohinder Singh
To be happily married / Mohinder Singh.
p. cm.
Includes index.
ISBN 9788178359762

1. Marriage--Miscellanea. I. Title.

DDC 306.81 23

Contents

Prologue 9

1. **Getting Married** 11

The Arranged Marriage • The Love Marriage • The Honeymoon.

2. **Couples at Work** 19

More Than Friends, Less Than Lovers • Sexual Harassment at the Workplace • Same-Company or Rival-Company Couples • Successful Wives, Threatened Husbands • Wives of Successful Men • Working Mothers • Working Fathers • Working from Home • When the Wife Outshines • Working Women's World • Men and Women at Work.

3. **Sex in Marriage** 53

Matters of Marital Sex • Spicing Marital Sex: Go Beyond 50/50 • Joy of Sex • Sex Life of Dual-Career Couples • Sexual Liveliness in Long Marriages • The Changing Pattern of Pornography • The TV Hug • Infidelity • Speaking of Adultery • Addicted to Sex.

4. **Money in Marriage** 75

Meaning of Money • Matters of Money • The Money Equation • Money and Happiness • Earn-and-Spend Syndrome.

5. **Children in Marriage** 87

Childless by Choice • The Only Child • Latecomers: Children Born to Older Parents • How Significant is Your Birth Order? • A First-Time Father • Choosing the Sex of Children • Suffering is Mostly for Women

• IVF (In Vitro Fertilization) • Sleepy Teenagers at School Time • Playing one Parent Against the Other • A Peep Into Parent–Offspring Conflict • Adolescent Impact on Marital Life • Parents Versus Peers in the Life of Teenagers • Devalued Dads • How Children React to TV Ads? • The Magic of the Family Meal • Picky Eating • Teenagers Driving.

6. **Married Couples Living in Joint Family** **129**

Mother-in-Law/Daughter-in-Law Relationships • Back Into the Empty Nest • How Good Are Grandparents? • Roles Reversed

7. **Healthcare in Marriage** **143**

Men and Women in Matters of Health • Husbands Who Neglect Their Health • Taking Your Medicine • Tired all the Time• Drinking Problems • Women and Excessive Drinking • Indoor Pollutants.

8. **Married Life in Middle Years** **159**

Married Life in Middle Age • Mulling Over the Middle Years • Staying Incompatible for Fifty Years • Retirement, a Second Marriage • Sex in Middle Years • Ageing Losses and Morale • Older People Tripping and Falling • Affluent Oldsters.

9. **What Makes a Marriage!** **179**

Secret of a Good Marriage • When Silence is Gold • One Secret of Happy Marriage: Separate Bathrooms • Dynamics of the Double Bed • The Wife's Birthday • Giving and Receiving of Gifts.

10. **What Mars a Marriage!** **191**

How do Men and Women Change in Marriage? • Coping with Clutter • The Family Slob • To Nag or Not to Nag • In Defence of the Marital Sulk • Forgetful Husbands • Are You Listening? • Husbands: An Irritating Form of Life • Couples in Cars.

11. Dealing with Our Differences **211**

How Muzzled are the Married? • A Few Wifely Likes and Dislikes • Are Men and Women Getting Mismatched? • Shopping : How Different with Women and Men!• The Deliverance of Divorce.

Epilogue 223

Index 225

Prologue

Marriage remains a popular subject of conversation and the one most written about. Yet the theme is well-nigh inexhaustible, as the conditions of living among people and places are ever in a flux. Here is another attempt at delineating the mystique of marriage by a husband and father who has observed and researched the institution with fascination for many years.

To be happily married is surely a blessing. Research worldwide has shown that couples who stay happily married live longer, suffer less stress, and are heir to fewer ailments as compared to those who are unhappily married or stay single.

Admittedly, luck plays a part in the choice of a partner. Yet a happy marriage involves much care and consideration on the part of the partners. It calls for a lifetime of patience, tolerance and goodwill between them. Besides a satisfactory sexual relationship, it requires everyday endearments and compliments between the two parties. Indeed, there could be no happy marriage unless the two continue to nurture respect for each other, respect for their intelligence, spirit of cooperation, efficiency and physical attraction. Giving of gifts, celebrating birthdays and occasional holiday trips do lend fun to a marriage.

Yet a marriage—more so a marriage in modern times—is not free from pitfalls. An obvious one is infidelity whose incidence could be rising with men and women working together in offices and other businesses. Dowry demands, more so when carried over years after marriage, can mar a union. Joint family living, wherever it is a part of married life, poses its own pluses and minuses. A partner not caring enough about his/her hygiene and health can be disturbing. Couples who drive can quarrel in cars about the style of driving and direction. Shopping together is another area where the male and female approach is often at variance. Children, especially adolescents, can create their own tension between the married.

With both husband and wife going out to work, the wife is prone to much stress unless the husband helps her in household chores. The question is often posed as to whether the "new man" has arrived, a man aware of his obligation to help his mate in running the house and the care of children.

Where both partners are earning money, the management of money becomes a crucial point in the smooth running of the marriage.

Married life in middle age poses its own problems, such as the 'empty nest', the return of adult children, and looking after aged dependents.

1

Getting Married

The Arranged Marriage

Arranged marriages through elders, family members, friends, acquaintances and family *pundits* have been the norm with us for centuries. For some years, these arrangements have been supplemented by matrimonial advertisements in papers, and now increasingly on matrimonial websites. In the latter, more information is made available about the person concerned and the family, often including a photograph of the prospective bride or groom.

Marriage continues to be a serious, solemn commitment with us, not only for the individuals involved but for their respective families, too. No wonder, most matrimonial advertisements emanate from parents and are formalized as offers of alliance between families.

The idealized bride-to-be! Who is she? And how has her image changed over the last few decades?

Some things have remained unchanged. The ideal persists that she should be young, beautiful, tall, slim, and fair.

Thirty years back the optimum age of a bride was 20 or just below—the age at which beauty queens get selected. With the emerging demand for brides with higher education, preferably professional, the same has moved up by a few years. Nevertheless, anyone pushing 30 has to do some explaining.

Beauty is the common denominator, both asked for and offered. Terms like 'very beautiful', 'extremely beautiful', and 'exceptionally beautiful' are not uncommon. And with boys mostly dubbed as 'handsome', that way we must be one of the most beautiful people on the planet!

The most popular epithet for girls used is 'homely', both demanded and offered. Surely, other aspects of her good nature are listed, such as 'amiable', 'affectionate', 'simple natured', 'sweet natured', 'soft-spoken', 'cooperative', 'sociable', 'cheerful', or 'perfect'. Yet the adjective 'homely' takes the cake. 'Homely' in the *Concise Oxford Dictionary* means "simple, primitive, unpretending". Americans are far harsher; the *New Webster's* defines it as "plain in appearance, unattractive". Yet, to us, the word 'homely' (taken as 'home-loving') symbolizes the very quintessence of what an Indian male and his family would want of the new bride—better, a *bahu*—someone for the whole family. At the minimum, it denotes a good homemaker, a devoted housewife, an obedient daughter-in-law and a would-be doting mother; in short, a giver, not a taker. And the homely part not to be pared down, irrespective of her being required to work outside to augment the family income.

Close on the heels of beauty comes education, the higher the better, preferably professional or technical with its surer potential for earning. Yet the 'open sesame' is still 'convent education'—popularly associated with a flare in social mixing and fluency in the English language.

Nowadays, a girl's job and income, or her potential for a career and earning, become as crucial to her marriage prospects as her looks and family.

Cases are not wanting where a couple under the arranged marriage could also have generated an element of love before wedlock itself.

The Love Marriage

The incidence of love marriages is on the rise, especially in our cities and towns. More and more girls are going into higher education, including professional courses like medicine, business management, architecture and so on. Again, greater numbers of women are working along with men in offices, stores, factories, hospitals and other places. Many a love match takes place between students in a medical college or in an architectural school or in business management courses. Even there have been love marriages between IAS probationers during their training course at the National Academy. Largely, urban girls are getting bolder in making marriage choices, sometimes in opposition to family opinion. In fact, there have been cases where the newlyweds are ostracized by their families.

The workplace, they say, is the best venue to meet a life partner. You can get to know one another unobtrusively, observe each other under stress, and so gain a good idea of a person's nature. In fact, some studies suggest that the workplace is already becoming the prime meeting ground where people find their mates, next only to matrimonial advertisements and marriage websites. The trend of late marriage has also meant more unmarried people in workplaces.

The spread of Facebook, Twitter and other social networks has added another dimension to love marriages.

In the Western world, another phenomenon has been afoot where couples live together without marriage. These live-in couples often stay unmarried for a year or more. Some times, the marriage is precipitated with the female getting pregnant or a baby being born. Again, there is the tradition of some live-in couples living together over long years.

Despite most marriages in the Western world being love marriages, and even some as live-in couples, around 50% marriages in the United States are currently ending in divorce. In that way, a love marriage does not automatically guarantee a durable union.

The live-in phenomenon is still quite uncommon in our country. Yet cases are cropping up, especially in cities, where a couple lives together without getting married. This trend could register a boost in line with what obtains in the West.

The Honeymoon

The word *honeymoon* comes from the idea that the first month of the marriage is the sweetest. The bridegroom particularly is said to be fed on honey, a highly nourishing food with no gastric complications.

Hints for the Groom

Unalloyed honeymoon bliss is more a fable than a fact. Sulks are as common as smiles; there can be even a few bridal sobs. That way there has been an over-selling of the honeymoon. Yet the myth survives strong. Expectations are high; it's 'the trip' of her life, an epic event in marriage.

The chances are yours is essentially an arranged marriage. Of course, you were consulted. You and your would-be wife met, possibly half a dozen times, with luck, once or twice in private. Physical intimacy is unknown.

Honeymoon advice—there sometimes seems more of it than is really wanted—will be forthcoming freely from friends and relatives. Do's and don'ts on the subject are galore. Yet a few camaraderie tips are herewith ventured if you care for more.

If you have the money, overseas honeymooning is the 'in' thing these days, first choice often being Europe and the United States. Travel agents helpfully sort out the itinerary and bookings.

It is perhaps best to venture abroad if you have been there before. Your envisaged role is that of an unerring guide, a leader-like senior; not a wide-eyed tourist lost in the wonderment of skyscrapers and supermarkets. The novelty of a different setting and the novelty of a marriage less than one week old can be at times too heady a mix.

Better avoid places, more so in the early phase of honeymoon, where English is not spoken. Nothing is as destructive of male vanity as the apparent helplessness to communicate around, to sort out things when one has lost one's way or the bride, her bag.

Leisurely walking amongst cheerful crowds in elegant walking streets will rarely fail to amuse your mate; the pair's private world cocooned in the midst of a lively, pulsating world—a sort of solitude in company. Exotic locations like the Lake

District or the Scottish moors could be left out for more settled marital days. And so, also, dragging her along to interminable picture galleries and museums.

Nearer home and cheaper (sometimes works out cheaper than an Indian holiday) are Kathmandu, Colombo, and Singapore. Kathmandu is a manageable place, with cheery residents and acceptable all-the-year weather. You can have the feel of a foreign currency, while your own is not despised—local casinos literally run on Indian rupees.

Our hill stations retain their pre-eminence as favoured honeymoon spots. Is it the escape from heat or from the din and dust of plains, or some scope to sit and walk outdoors in comparative privacy? Honeymooners streaming into hill station hotels; all going to do the same thing, the lobby clerk knows and the bellboy knows.

Better, you stay at the best hotel even if you have to raise a loan for it. Besides comfort and privacy, you are required to display style, possibly your last independent chance of doing so. Be generous with tips.

Incidentally, whenever you stir out for a longish hill walk, better keep in your shoulder bag a pair of sturdy canvas shoes for her along with soft thick socks. This can earn you an unbelievable amount of goodwill when she starts hobbling footsore in her new shoes.

Seaside resorts are gaining popularity. Goa has particularly much to recommend itself. Yet seaside stays suffer one small snag. Newly nuptial brides are often too bashful to bare themselves in bikinis, more so in the open, to take full advantage of sun and sand.

Prolonged train or road journeys could best be avoided in the first few days. Better save the hassles of frequent packing and unpacking; the first marital quarrel is often about some item that is misplaced or left behind.

A golden rule: in planning every trip and programme: allow a wide margin of time. Your pushing and hurrying could be somewhat frightening or someone unused to your ways. In any case, she needs more time to get ready and organize herself than you normally anticipate.

It is better to stick to standard and tried food and drink, risking little experimentation. Roadside *chaats* and uncertain tinned stuff is not for you. Your most inglorious scenario would be an upset rumbling stomach emitting embarrassing sounds, if nothing worse.

Carry a handy bottle of whisky or brandy if a peg or two peps you up. However, to get drunk on a honeymoon, to create a nuisance or pass out, is an unforgivable sin, next only to going off with another woman.

This is not an occasion to dilate on the 'facts of life'. She's all yours, yet do not rush things.

Watch your words, even more than your actions (action you can blame on somebody, your words are your own). Stay wary of dowry discussions, if you have not already jeopardized marital happiness by dowry demands.

There is no use recalling wistfully your bachelor days. Most women do not have the remotest notion of the conviviality of bachelor evenings. Your best bet is to talk of the future—joint hopes and joint wishes—than of each other's past.

If you have not enough time for a full-fledged honeymoon, better go in for a mini-moon.

Mohan and Reena had planned an elaborate two-week honeymoon in Bali. However, Mohan Khosla, a leading Delhi advocate, is saddled with a case that needs his regular presence for the next thirty days. And Reena, running her own gynaecology clinic, is finding difficult to arrange a substitute. So rather than heading for Bali, the Khoslas did something decidedly less romantic. They drove to the Sariska Palace Hotel, a 2-hour-drive from Delhi, to unwind themselves for a 3-day weekend.

The couple waited until everything settled down. They took their own time to plan an extensive honeymoon to an exotic place of their choice. They toiled through the winter months on their grueling work schedule. Only after four months of their mini-moon, did they manage to go on their dream holiday to Bali for a fortnight. And they had a glorious honeymoon there.

Was it worth the wait? "Definitely," says Mohan. "We would not have enjoyed it as much if we'd gone right after the wedding." And Reena nods in agreement.

Hints for the Bride

Evidently, it is mainly the responsibility of the groom to make the honeymoon a success. At this stage of marriage, he is supposed to provide the needed leadership. Yet brides have to do their bit to make the honeymoon a pleasant phase. The best is to support your partner's ego—the thing he would be prizing most at this stage of marriage.

Happily, Indian girls, particularly in cities, are increasingly getting surer of themselves and cling to fewer hang-ups than before.

Of course, the honeymoon adjustments become easier where the partners are familiar with each other before wedlock.

2

Couples at Work

More Than Friends, Less Than Lovers

As the workplace becomes increasingly open to women, there's more and more mingling of the sexes at work. A question often pondered if not actually asked: Can men and women in the workplace continue as friends—without slipping into relationships as lovers? Some pose an even more basic question: Can men and women be friends?

And this gets support from Don O'Meara at the University of Cincinnati. O'Meara, however, finds four principal challenges to male–female friendship: defining it, dealing with sexual attraction, seeing each other as equals, and facing people's responses to the relationship.

Earlier, two management trainers, David R. Eyler and Andreas P. Baridon, attempted a relationship model for the American workplace. It pictured a positive way for men and women to share intimate feelings outside of marriage or an illicit affair. And it rejected the traditional saint or sinner model of colleague relationship as too simplistic for modern life.

Social scientists, however, concede that the field of research on this aspect is still in its infancy. Only now they are beginning to understand some basic truths about male–female friendship.

A new scenario is surely emerging at workplaces: women in increasing numbers working side by side with men. This daily physical proximity between the genders, more so when joined with the stimulation of shared work, brings with it the likelihood of sexual attraction.

Another factor favouring sexual attraction among colleagues is the fact of their being of the same age, similar socio-economic background, similar values and similar aspirations. And today's work in many offices and businesses can mean irregular hours, non-office settings and the greater intimacy of business travel.

Already society is undergoing its awkward adjustment to the phenomenon of working wives. To it is added the complication of women interacting day-long with other men, which offers countless opportunities for working friendships to develop. "Even the most secure people in a strong marriage probably don't want a spouse to be establishing a new friendship, especially with someone who's very attractive," says Prof. Raymond Monsour.

Eyler and Baridon call this relationship "non-sexual love". And find that women seem to have an intuitive grasp of the same. They're the ones who usually move to forge it, often out of the wreckage of a colleague's attempt at something sexual—the way some of our women project a brother–sister relationship, often aided by rakhi-tying. Men usually have a difficult time adjusting to the idea. They find it harder to give up the deeply ingrained macho model of a sexual conquest.

Admittedly, sexual attraction among certain co-workers is inevitable. And some persons will pursue sexual attraction to have affairs or with a view to marriage. But the vast majority would neither be interested in a commitment like marriage, especially if already married, nor an affair that has the potential to disrupt their career or established relationships. For such persons, Eyler and Baridon envisage a unique new relationship that is limited to sharing personal revelations and intimacy, but not sharing bodies: mutual respect and communication as an alternative to the old game of seduction and conquest.

The two trainers advocate this new sexual etiquette for those who wish to exploit the energy of workplace attraction without physical sex or falling in love, or the other extreme of avoiding each other altogether and pretending that the workplace is genderless. And they make a few suggestions that can pull off the new relationship—more than friends, less than lovers.

You have to establish boundaries and expectations for the right relationship. The parties are enjoined to discuss openly and decide what is and is not off-limits. Some boundaries, notably the sexual one, they agree never to cross. Similarly, neither physical contact nor the language of lovers has a place in the relationship, as these will only send wrong signals.

Without a conscious management of the proposed relationship, personal attraction can lead to destructive consequences. Differences have to be resolved openly, instead of letting them fester in ambiguity. Initially, it may be difficult to discuss emotional issues of the new relationship, but these should be brought into the open for honest discussion, when you sense some tension building up. Two people seldom approach a relationship with perfectly matched expectations. And so the necessity to remove misunderstandings from time to time. Over time, the power of sexual attraction is not diminished, but the two involved gain more experience and skill in handling it.

The workplace relationship has one advantage over marriage relationship: in the former you can have periods of cooling-off if things seem like going out of hand. And you are not obliged to take care of each other or to tolerate differences on daily basis as in marriage.

Where the new relationship succeeds, it can lead to more creativity in work. There's a magic between 'business couples' that makes their work exciting. They do genuinely inspired work together; their creative energy flowing from a sexual attraction they've chosen not to indulge in physically or force into love.

According to Eyler and Baridon, the relationship advocated by them is largely workable. The days of insecure spouses who waited at home has passed; part of the revolution that has swept women into jobs. Peers now understand peers. Colleagues may be sometimes tempted to become lovers, but many more may settle for being friends than lovers.

And the two trainers discuss a few myths of man–woman attraction. For example, it is believed that a red-blooded heterosexual male is incapable of spending long periods of time with an attractive woman worker without making sexual advances. That's why it's considered risky for men and women to work alone together after office hours. Yes, men admit that they can't control the feeling, but deny that it leads them to hit on every attractive female within their orbit. Similarly, it is commonly believed that if work partners are sexually attracted, they can't possibly do the job effectively—their minds will be on sex rather than on work. That's why a management often feels obliged to break a team where it suspects sexual attraction. But then, sexual energy, if kept within bounds, can stimulate creativity and work drive.

"The belief that men and women can't be friends comes from another era in which women were at home and men were in the workplace, and the only way they could get together was for romance," explains Linda Sapadin, Ph.D., a noted psychologist in New York. "Now they work together and sport interests together and socialize together." Of course, it's tricky—society has long singled out romance as the prototypical male-female relationship. And the reality that physical attraction could suddenly enter the equation of cross-sex friendship uninvited is always lurking in the background.

The obstacles may seem numerous and formidable, yet male–female friendship is becoming not only a possibility but also a necessity. If men and women are to work, play and co-exist in modern society, researchers believe that men and women must learn to understand and communicate with each other. To Kathy Werking, author of *We're Just Good Friends* (Guilford, 1997), "of pairs that do face the question of lust, those who decide early on to bypass an uncertain romantic relationship are more likely to have an enduring friendship".

Yet voices aren't wanting that alert people against getting into emotional involvement with workmates of the opposite gender, even while abjuring sex. According to them, emotional dependency on someone other than your marital partner almost amounts to infidelity, notwithstanding the absence of sex.

Anyway when your friend's feelings become more important than those of your spouse, it should ring alarm bells.

Whatever the challenges of male–female friendship, researchers agree that to succeed as friends, both genders have to openly and honestly negotiate exactly what their relationship will mean. If sex is part of the problem, addressing it explicitly is deemed the best strategy.

How relevant is the "new relationship" to our Indian conditions is hard to say. It could be made out that our social, cultural and work scenario isn't identical with the Western. Yet human beings everywhere are the same. With growing interaction between sexes in the country's modern workplaces, the phenomenon of male–female relationship therein calls for study and understanding. It would do no good to ignore it or push it under the carpet.

Sexual Harassment at the Workplace

With both married partners going out for work, the question of the wife having a hassle-free work environment assumes some importance. A wife suffering from repeated sexual harassments in the office would have her peace of mind disturbed. And this in turn could interfere with the peacefulness of a marriage.

In this context, an opportunity is taken to comment on the sexual harassment scene in offices and other workplaces.

On August 13, 1997, a bench of the Supreme Court of India headed by the Chief Justice gave a landmark judgment, elaborating that fundamental rights encompassed gender equality, including prevention of sexual harassment or abuse. The court enjoined on employers, both government and private, to ensure that women do not work in "hostile" work environment, whether caused by employees or outsiders.

The court defined sexual harassment as "such unwelcome sexually determined behaviour (whether directly or by implication) as physical contact and advances, a demand or request for sexual favours, sexually coloured remarks, showing pornography and any other unwelcome physical, verbal or non-verbal conduct of sexual nature." And it laid down that until government came up with the requisite legislation, these directives of the court would be binding and enforceable in law.

Urged by the public outcry on Nirbhaya case, the Central government has promptly putting legislation granting further protection to women, particularly against stalking, molesting and other forms of sexual overtures. Wherever enforced, this will give relief to our women workers against harassment by office Romeos.

The latest judgment of the apex court is in line with the law and standards developed in the United States over the last two decades. Sexual harassment at the work place, more so lately in the armed forces, continues to be the subject of intense debate in that country. Something like 1000 studies are published each year on the subject in reputable journals alone.

Sexual harassment in itself is not new; women have been harassed at work ever since they worked alongside men. Traditionally, it took the shape of employers/superiors giving or promising something in exchange for sexual favours. On the other hand, in reverse, some loss in company benefits inflicted or threatened for withholding sexual favours. Moreover, this kind of sexual harassment still figures widely.

However, with more and more women coming into the workforce, other forms of sexual harassment by colleagues, even juniors, is on the rise: lecherous looks—"eyes ever fixed at chest level", sexual jokes and innuendoes, touching and rubbing, asking questions of a personal nature, and so on. Possibly, nurses and policewomen fare worse than others. Sexual harassment has been likened to "the dripping tap"—small, mundane, accumulating. Many a man indulging in it stays blissfully unaware of its harmful effects, treating it more as a form of fun.

During the 1980 and 1990, a new legal concept of sexual harassment took shape: the concept of a hostile work environment. This is essentially an offshoot of the full equality extended to women vis-à-vis men at the workplace. Any sexual harassment that makes women employee feel uncomfortable, lose her concentration, lower her self-confidence, and otherwise interfere with her efficient functioning becomes illegal.

American courts have now determined that an office environment to be judged hostile would be from the standards of "a reasonable woman", and not "a reasonable person". And the aggrieved has not to prove a psychological injury; merely feeling uncomfortable could be enough. Even a male colleague can complain, on the scope of being offended by the vulgar comments or gestures of his fellow males towards women in the workplace.

Yet the most important development of all: courts have set out in unambiguous terms the obligation of an employer to provide working conditions free of sexual harassment. Employers have been held liable for the behavior of non-employees—the mailman, the copier repairman or a client. A number of restaurant owners have been successfully sued for not providing requisite protection to their waitresses from abuse by patrons. Even the failure of an employer to investigate properly a complaint of sexual harassment has been assumed as tacit support to gender discrimination. Ordinarily, a complaint must be acted upon within twenty-four hours of its being received.

Suits on sexual harassment have multiplied. More money is reportedly paid, prompted by threats of sexual harassment suits than actual award by courts. Insurance companies have started offering insurance cover against such suits. Consultants are busy holding seminars on the subject, and training material is selling briskly.

At one time Europeans were rather amused at the emerging American scene. To many of them, Americans were carrying the matter too far. Critics feared that carried to excess, it could make men avoid friendly banter with women colleagues. And this could also hurt the chances of marriages coming through between people at the same workplace. "How can a man get anywhere with a woman without harassing her?" says a wit.

However, by now, the countries of EEC and several others have enacted similar laws and codes. Firms are designating senior members of the staff as "advisors" and giving them some training about monitoring sexual harassment and hearing informal complaints. And so also a prescribed procedure is required for formal complaints. Major firms often issue a policy paper on the subject. Many corporate houses now see sexual harassment as bad for business. Some companies have stopped holding office Christmas parties—occasions notorious for bingeing and unwanted flirtations. Others are considering the legality of banning dating among co-workers. Employers, big and small, are taking energetic steps to combat sexual harassment, more to avoid expensive judicial awards against them.

School boards and university authorities are designating senior faculty members to recognize acts of sexual harassment and take necessary action to ensure that such instances are addressed quickly, fairly and effectively.

The Indian scene is still to be surveyed in depth but there is every indication that the incidence of sexual harassment at workplaces is fairly high. And it may well be on the rise with more women coming into the workforce. Only the modalities of sexual harassment can be somewhat different from what obtains in the West.

Everywhere women sexually harassed at work are hesitant to complain about it. But in India, particularly, most victims still prefer to bear it in silence than to make a complaint. Evidently, this stems from the fear of losing the job itself, getting transferred, or inviting other reprisals. In any other case, a complaint can bring much unwelcome notoriety, even blame for any possible encouragement in the first place.

Section 354 of the Indian Penal Code ('outraging the modesty of a woman') and Section 509 of IPC ('insulting the modesty of a woman') do serve their purpose but are not designed to afford specific relief from the invidious day-to-day sexual harassment that takes place at workplaces.

The latest judgment of the Supreme Court now provides the needed lead. The court has opted for an approach that has been fairly successful elsewhere. It is now for the government to legislate in detail.

Possibly, a time has also come to set up a special agency to monitor sexual harassment in workplaces. Maybe we can model it on the Equal Employment Opportunity Commission

(EEOC) of America. EEOC directly hears complaints as well as issues guidelines from time to time on the subject of sexual harassment. And its guidelines are deemed as binding.

Egged on by the court and the forces of modernization, Indian businesses and even government departments have started taking steps against sexual harassment on their premises. To that extent, husbands are getting a little more relaxed about wives working in offices.

The Indian government is now legislating on the protection of women from sexual harassment at workplaces, mainly on the guidelines laid down by the Supreme Court.

Same-Company or Rival-Company Couples

A newly-married couple is working in the same software company as programmers. In fact, the two were working in the same jobs before they got married. Now they form a same-company couple.

Of late, there has been a rising curve in numbers of same-company couples. A firm initially recruiting a couple is uncommon but people working in the same place come together, fall in love, get married. And these marriages are mostly between persons holding equivalent positions, between persons having similar social and educational backgrounds.

Same-company couples could confer some advantages on the company: greater cooperation between them and smoother work-sharing. Yet they also give rise to a few administrative complications for the management. Take performance appraisal. Two employees joined in matrimony are rarely clones. One is generally more competent, more astute, more useful than the other. Appraisals, sensitive placing and raises will be different for each.

But any differentiation at company level can make one partner disgruntled, more so if the person left behind is the husband. Even otherwise, one dissatisfied partner can sour the relations of both with the company.

There's the added complication if one partner has to submit work to the other. Managers are not sure—and co-workers have their own fears—whether the supervisory role of one partner over the other will be carried out without fear or favour.

Time was when employees, like soldiers, moved whenever and wherever the company wanted to send them. Getting someone to move anywhere these days is a formidable task. Even nonworking-wife couples resist displacement. Those with children must seek out appropriate schools for them.

Transferring one half of a dual-career couple can meet with far greater resistance.

All office politics rest on the assumption that each person thinks and acts as an individual. What makes it difficult for couples is that they are often treated as one unit. This can be particularly frustrating for the pair when it comes to information gathering.

Co-workers are usually hesitant to tell one partner anything they don't want the other partner to know. The assumption is that at home all pillow talk is work-related. This is largely a false assumption; couples talk of other things most of the time.

There was this IAS couple of the same seniority serving the same state (quite a few IAS are now marrying batch-mates). The wife happened to hold the post of Appointments Secretary. Colleagues couldn't help wondering whether her husband would come to know of various transfer proposals in advance, even learn about his own Confidential Roll kept in her custody. In real life, his chances of becoming privy to his Roll through his wife were minimal. Yet the couple couldn't escape a suspicious air about it.

Couples working in rival companies face another set of problems. Luckily such pairing is still the exception.

Here are couples who stay in the same house, sleep in the same bed, eat at the same table, but go out every day to work for companies that are sworn and bitter enemies, such as Pepsi Cola and Coca Cola.

For some, especially those in higher positions, the situation can be quite stressful. So couples work out their own coping strategies.

Often a ground rule is operated that anything said within the house will be just between them. Banning all talk of work is simply impracticable; human beings are human beings. Something will slip, or they'll say something. There's no point their saying, "We're not going to talk of anything related to work". What they must agree is that whatever they talk about has not to go outside the house.

Companies are a little chary of sharing all their secrets with an employee whose spouse is working with a competing company. This is something that doesn't do justice to rival-company couples but that's possibly the price they have to pay for the unusual situation in which they find themselves. They have to display extra loyalty and zest to win the trust of their employers.

Successful Wives, Threatened Husbands

I know a couple, both in the IAS, with the wife three years junior to him in service. In the early years of their marriage, he mostly managed prestigious postings while she struggled through some routine ones along with bearing two children and handling their upbringing. Now his career has suffered a setback—both due to his mistakes and some bad luck—while she has lately blossomed into a powerful top bureaucrat.

What's fascinating is the different ways they have been reacting to changing fortunes in their service careers. When he was up and she was down, she seemed genuinely glad for him and boasted to everyone about how well he was doing. When the roles lie reversed he sulks, even moves party conversation away from her latest achievements to things like political corruption or fighting in Afghanistan.

Of course, if confronted with this he is bound to remonstrate horrified. "I'm really proud of my wife's success," he enthuses. But this may be more to keep up appearances. Actually, he seems more threatened than thrilled by her success, and it keeps on breaking out in his behaviour.

This is not an isolated case. Husbands may make out that they are thrilled by their partners' achievements but the truth is that many of them often feel threatened by their successful spouses. And the threat is perceived greater where the wife excels in the same sphere as the husband; her excelling in an altogether different sphere, especially in a womanly sphere, is less threatening. Men passively resist and emotionally withdraw from wives who have become confident and apparently independent. Being married to a powerful and successful man enormously enhances a woman's status, but the reverse is not necessarily true.

Why is it somewhat hard for men to genuinely glorify in the achievements of their women? Possibly it is a question of identity. So much of male self-esteem seems to be tied up in the public acknowledgement of them as winners and leaders. If the woman they are married to is recognized by society as equally, or even more successful, they see themselves as automatically relegated to the second spot. The situation is all the more galling where the man is going through a bad patch in his own career.

Two-career marriages are essentially a new phenomenon that has come into prominence in the last few decades. Husbands love the double income these generate and so actively seek partners with jobs. Yet it will take some time for men—nursed in the traditional roles—to get adjusted to the realities of a truly equal marriage and the shifting balance of power in relationships. In the meantime, it can be a real assault on a man's ego if his wife earns more than he or holds a more prestigious position; society still defines men by their earning ability. And such situations won't be uncommon in the coming years.

Besides the hurt to ego, what's at the root of men's antipathy towards successful wives is their fear of abandonment. "My wife won't look after my food and clothes. She won't bear my child except in her own good time. She does not need my money. She is not even keen to carry my name. She does not rely on me any more." It goes back to his basic fear of being abandoned by another female—his mother.

When husbands begin harbouring the impression that their wives care more for their careers than for them, it can develop backlash in marriage. And this can take a lot of forms—criticism of her household work, sabotaging her professional aspirations, pushing childbirth on her when she is not ready for it, refusing to help in household chores, physical and emotional abuse, withholding affection, an inordinate demand for sex, having an affair with a more passive woman. A few go to the extent of forcing their working wife to choose between her husband and her job. Usually the wife's work triggers greater hostility if it involves her coming late from office or travelling outside.

Men with working wives are sometimes known to take their rage out on their female colleagues. Others seek solace in relying overtly on their female secretaries; a sort of emotional substitute for the perceived loss of nurturing at home by their working wives.

With more and more women joining the workforce, the traditional concept of marriage is set to undergo a radical change. But like most of other social changes, the process can be quite painful, particularly to men. Eventually, one hope, a new ideology of marriage would take shape—more companionate and more sharing. Its hallmark will be the greater equality of women, with most women working and men taking their share of household chores. In this scenario, a successful wife should not be as threatening to the male ego as it is often now.

Wives of Successful Men

Kamla invariably experienced a feeling of rising unease and a wildly thumping heart whenever she was obliged to preside over some social function, her husband being the vice-chairman of an automobile manufacturing company. And she bordered on panic when playing hostess to a group of his business colleagues.

Kamla dreaded the prospect of making the customary speech at any award presenting ceremony. And at business dinners, she worried no end about her inadequacy in making appropriate conversation. Now such occasions were getting more frequent with the opening up of the automobile industry and its growing globalization.

Not to mention men, she found other wives often better informed about business matters, let alone those who had careers of their own. No wonder Kamla hunted for excuses not to participate in corporate functions and was mercifully relieved if one of her ruses worked. "A child was ill." "I was too tired."

She was educated all right—a graduate, and brought up in a family of professionals. However, on marriage, she had principally concentrated on her home and bringing up the three children, while her ambitious husband, Harish, was busily climbing up the corporate ladder.

Like many old-time wives, Kamla could have resigned herself to a quiet existence, allowing Harish to lead a separate, independent life outside the home. But such withdrawal, she felt, spelled defeat, a sure recipe for self-loathing. Wasn't it a sin to waste the days of God's beautiful life in self-hate? And then there was the lurking fear that Harish might exchange her for a 'trophy' wife—a smart young belle brimming with self-confidence and highly supportive of his career.

So, at forty, she took up the challenge of an executive wife. She began to study other people at all the social functions she attended. Watching and listening, she learned quite a few fascinating things. For example, she found that the best hostesses always appeared to be genuinely interested in their guests—all of them. They had a way of encouraging people to talk about themselves, and made mental notes regarding their guests' interests and comments. And then recalled those remarks during future meetings. It proved an instant conversation starter.

Life, it became apparent to her, was all about our approach to people—making friends, knowing business acquaintances and building business relationships. And here, some strategies worked surprisingly well: always a smile when being introduced, asking questions about others' lives and interests, and always listening intently to what was being said.

As Kamla gained in confidence as an executive wife—

confidence breeding more confidence, she also sought professional advice on how to become the powerful influence behind her successful husband. She shed some weight and changed her hair style. Even started taking interest in the golf talk of her husband and his playing cronies. Her transformation within a few years from a diffident, poorly informed housewife to an effectively helpful mate in business surprised everybody, more so Harish.

No one can quantify the worth of a corporate wife. New-style bosses believe the right wife creating the right ambience can genuinely oil the wheels of business. Whereas business deals were often clinched between men only, wives are now required to entertain and woo potential and existing clients. Cynics say the present trend to include wives is simply a way of keeping the ladies happy.

However, if a woman decides to become part of her husband's business life, then it is far better to make this decision early and to tackle the situation head-on. Nowadays, with a few exceptions, most well-known, high-flying executives have wives who back them all the way. They are well-presented, well informed and act as perfect hostesses. They could well miss a few desirable things such as a relaxed home life or some vocation of their own, but then the rewards of an executive wife are great. Being a corporate wife is wonderful! It can be exciting, alluring, glamorous, challenging or powerful. There is travel, entertainment, and the excitement of meeting new people and solving novel problems.

Her role is no longer merely ceremonial. She must be able to tell time in important world cities, have some idea of exchange rates, feel comfortable in foreign cultures and mix well with corporate hierarchy.

She is expected to know a good deal about her husband's company, even when she doesn't work alongside him. And something about that industry itself and the major competitors. If called upon to entertain company's clients, she takes care to inform herself beforehand about basic particulars of their interests and their families. It has to be understood that no business social function is for entertainment purposes alone.

It is always a public relations exercise designed to promote goodwill, with the eventual aim of increasing business.

It must be said that a good percentage of younger wives are now taking the initiative and are going ahead with being a "good company wife". They realize that if they have not got the required skills already, these can be learned. Here, professional help can minimize the travails of trial and error.

Working Mothers

A working mother has two clusters of duties, household and job, both of which were traditionally considered as full-time occupations. And the question is not solely one of the amount of time and energy needed for the two; there are special conflicts when the woman has simultaneous responsibilities in her home and at her place of employment. Even a different set of behaviours may be called for: competitive and assertive in the office, cooperative and nurturing at home.

Considerable concern has, therefore, been evinced about the health and well-being of the working mother. Numerous surveys and studies have been carried out about the effects of this dual role on the working mothers. Some of the findings from such studies and researches are discussed below.

Effect on Physical Health

Employed mothers as a group appear healthier than housewives. Possibly, the difference may be due to selective recruitment of healthier mothers into employment or a tendency of those whose health is poor to leave employment. Still, the difference favouring the employed suggests that the dual set of role responsibilities is not typically damaging to the health of the mother; the earlier apprehensions about it have proved ill-founded.

The working mothers clearly report fewer physical symptoms than mothers who do not work. Even the average blood pressure is almost identical between the two categories. Of course, this finding should not be applied to all women as individuals. Some jobs and some in combination with particular household responsibilities would be taxing for some women.

Yet today, and presumably even more in the future, there seems to be no basis for a general concern about the health of employed mothers. Does employment tend to improve health? An interesting question that would require more research to answer.

Effect on Psychological Health

Concern about combining full-time employment with adequate performance in child care and housekeeper roles seems to have been extremely widespread among employed mothers. However, employed mothers are not the only ones to have problems with anxiety and guilt. Some studies showed that full-time college-educated housewives were actually more anxious and overall concerned about their children than comparable women who combined a professional career with motherhood.

Again, whatever anxiety and guilt working mothers may have experienced, it was rarely translated into symptoms like sleeplessness or nervousness. In fact, some studies have revealed the opposite. Employed mothers are more likely to be free of such symptoms; good mental–emotional health has been reported for a larger proportion of professionally employed wives than equally able full-time housewives. And employed mothers have more positive image of themselves than the mere housewives.

Effect on Recreation

The image of the employed mother as a harried person suggests less time available for recreation. Some activities—especially those that require large blocks of day-time hours, such as card-playing, TV viewing, gossiping and visiting in the neighbourhood—get reduced considerably. Entertaining is lessened. In addition to requiring considerable time, formal entertaining requires advance planning and commitments, which may be difficult for the employed woman and her family.

Studies, particularly of American working mothers, however, showed that neither the family recreation (except TV viewing) nor commercial recreation (except golf) was appreciably affected. Recreation enjoyed a higher priority with working mothers than had been suspected. Mothers seem to have retained those recreational patterns that were meaningful to them, such as joint activities with their families and kin, and things like dancing, movies and active physical sports.

Effects on Children

The earlier view that maternal employment had greater effects on the child, all bad, is not supported by recent research. Yes, effects it has but these depend on the nature of the employment, the attitude of the mother, her family circumstances, social class, the age and sex of the child, the kind of child-care arrangements, and a host of other conditions. Juvenile delinquency, for example, increased in lower classes with maternal employment, but remained unaffected by maternal employment in the middle class. Incidentally, the working mother is milder in discipline because of conscious effort to compensate or because of higher morale.

Both male and female students with employed mothers perceived significantly smaller differences between men and women. Daughters of working women, particularly, saw women as competent and effective. They viewed work as something they will want to do when they are mothers. Daughters of women in high-status occupations held the most forward views about male–female equality.

The idea that maternal employment brings emotional deprivation to the school-age child has not been supported in most studies. Of course, the absence of negative effects does not mean that mother's employment is irrelevant to the child; possibly mothers have been sufficiently concerned to effectively counterbalance any ill effects. Studies suggest that the working mother who obtains personal satisfaction from employment, does not have excessive guilt, and has adequate housekeeping arrangements. She is likely to perform as the nonworking mother or even better for her school-going children.

The effects of maternal employment on the infant depends on the extent of the mother's absence and the nature of the substitute care—whether it is warm, stimulating and stable. However, while studies on maternal employment and the school-age child offer reassurance to the working mother, no such reassurance is forthcoming concerning the impact on infants.

Husband–Wife Relationship

Employed wives tend to have greater power than non-employed wives. Whereas housewives relative to working wives are more powerful in internal household affairs, working wives have relatively greater external power, particularly with regard to financial matters. The most consistent finding from the studies in which various decision areas were examined, is the positive association between the wife's employment and her power concerning financial matters.

Studies indicate greater marital happiness for those wives who take employment voluntarily, because such opportunity extends their freedom of choice. On the other hand, being forced into taking employment reduces their autonomy and results in lessened marital satisfaction.

Apparently, the advantages associated with employment compensated for the higher levels of conflicts faced in their marriages. Yet, on the composite score, nonworking wives of husbands with high income, ranked the highest in marital satisfaction.

Working Fathers

Rajiv, a sales officer in a major manufacturing group, is working under stress today. Not the usual work stress, but something that's termed DaddyStress. His 4-year-old son had his periodic bout of asthma this morning. The boy had to be left in the care of a live-in maid; the mother works in a bank. Pawan's distraught face as he saw his parents leaving for work has been haunting Rajiv during the day. To others around, he's a man at work but he can't help worrying about the sick kid back home.

In popular parlance, 'working mother' has come to symbolize conflict; the constant tug-of-war between her 'job self' and 'parent self'. She's pictured as the harried one, always juggling her time and attention between the demands of office and home.

Coupled to it is the common assumption that working fathers are largely immune from such conflicts. How valid is this assumption? New studies in the West on working fathers have brought to light a rising undercurrent of DaddyStress, a largely unrecognized conflict between the double duties of work and family.

Not that men—more so, working fathers—are slackening their interest in work and careers. Indeed, men most eager for increased work challenge and responsibility happen to be fathers of young children. Yet these men are tending to display a high level of simultaneous commitment to both work and family.

It seems the traditional role-model of a 'good father' is undergoing a change. A modern one has not only to be a good provider but also to be involved in his children's daily life. Take baby care. Once it was mainly the province of mothers. Now fathers are moving into infant care and feeding. And they are accepting greater responsibility for the care of a sick or injured child. The phenomenon is evidently more pronounced in dual-career nuclear families. In the domestic domain itself, the labour gap between working mothers and fathers is narrowing significantly.

Contrary to common belief, men also display marked physical and emotional reactions when concerned about their children's well-being. In an experiment conducted by Michael Lamb, a New York researcher, parents' blood pressure, heart rate, and galvanic skin response were monitored while exposing them to their crying baby. It was found that there was no difference in reaction between mothers and fathers.

Of course, men generally don't express their emotions about parenthood as readily as women. It is indeed a 'man-thing' not to talk about work–family conflict. Various cultural cues tend to keep men quiet about their family needs and obligations. For example, in most cultures, men would hesitate to take paternity leave (even when paid paternity leave is admissible) for fear of peer ridicule. And many men would prefer to take sick leave for themselves rather than admitting their need to be at home to look after a sick child. It is not just the fear of compromising their jobs that leads men to keep their dual responsibility invisible. It's from fear of compromising their myth of masculinity that many men hide their family concerns from friends and colleagues.

Yet work and family are interdependent spheres for fathers, just as these are for mothers. Each aspect of their life deeply affects the other. Men under acute Daddy Stress are likely to make more mistakes at work as there is a certain loss of concentration.

Working from Home

In pre-industrial times, people who worked at crafts in their own cottages had a more integrated pattern of work and living. This pattern broke up with the advent of industrial revolution. Much activity shifted to factories and offices. People went out to work and often stayed away from their home for the whole day.

Well, there are indications this may be getting reversed. The home–office movement seems to be picking up, more so in post-industrial settings. Here, technology is playing a crucial part in the shape of the personal computer, Internet, scanners, printers, photocopier and mobile phones. The home can now provide its inhabitants with much of the information and services they need to run a professional business. Further, there is the present-day trend towards a certain decentralization of work, and this permits people to once again work from their homes.

As a result, the number of home-based consultants and professionals is rising fast. There is the attraction of a closer family life, and some relief from the hassles of commuting at peak traffic hours. Many are opting out for the arrangement from the cost angle; apparently it's cheaper to operate from home than to hire a downtown office and service it.

A decision to work from home is not a simple one; it has its own complex ramifications. It will alter the pace and texture of your days. And it will bring into the domestic zone of home and family the strictures and imperatives of the work zone. That way, two contrasting zones do overlap: the home standing for nurturing and recuperation, the workplace denoting productivity and aggression.

So, steps have to be taken to see that each is preserved or enhanced, not diminished. An important strategy is to separate the work zone physically from the rest of the house—some semblance of the old separation between the home and work zones, but in the home itself. Preferably, using a basement or *barsati* if a separate self-contained section is not feasible on the ground floor. Yet it is often the psychological separation that is harder to manage than the physical.

It is a somewhat different situation where the wife works from home—more to the liking of husbands. A wife working from home does not have to keep such a strict separation between the two zones. In fact, her presence at home makes it easier for her to oversee the household functioning and the care of children. Yet such a situation usually leaves her overburdened and overanxious; the men folk are apt to expect the same standard of household service as if she was not working. Possibly, her life is a little easier when she works from home with her husband.

While working from home grants the advantage of being near one's kids, this proximity produces its own conflicts. Where should the children play, or where should they not play? When can they use the phone, or when they can't? When can you be interrupted in your work, or what constitutes a real emergency? In a sense, you are competing to gain an environment previously all devoted to domestic pursuits. Another risk: you may start treating your spouse or a kid as an employee, ordering them about, at least expecting a supportive role from them.

To change over from working in an office to working from home, you require some behavioural reorientation. It is a change from the competitive psychology of workplace to the relatively undirected behaviour of home life. You can do without a strict observance of office hours like from 9 to 5, but there have to be definite goals and deadlines, albeit self-chosen and self-imposed yet no less rigorous. Otherwise, the temptation of periodic snacks, the call of cricket matches on TV, the voices of children playing, and occasional street disturbances can easily derail the most diligent home-worker.

There is also the opposite risk: that of work from home usurping far too much of one's time and attention—eating into most of leisure time or giving a feeling as if one is never "off" work. Things like starting with the phone as one wakes up or keeping up with it at meal times.

There are no easy solutions to these distortions. You may swing back and forth between under-work and overwork until experience teaches you a sensible balance.

Who works best at home? If you are contemplating starting a home business, first ask yourself a few questions. Do you like working alone? Home business can produce a sense of isolation particularly if you have a small family or none, or if you have no assistants. In that event, it is good to get out of the house as a regular part of the work routine.

There is the real risk of failure in any sort of entrepreneurial venture, especially when you are doing it alone. Sure, there will be difficulties—financial uncertainties, not to mention a host of other problems. The cost of failure can also be high, both psychologically and financially. You have to be good to survive. That way only one's own little business affords one a sense of discovering, what high quality in work means. This assumes things like 'good' at marketing decisions as well as producing a product, good at selecting help for invoicing and accounting, trafficking jobs, and customer relations, etc.

No doubt, it takes something extra to turn your back on paid employment and to start on one's own. As a group, home-workers display a remarkable belief in themselves and in the future. Much of the homeward migration these days is being led by optimistic, self-confident people.

More people currently are using their home offices as extensions of their corporate desks than for any other purpose. It is estimated that in another 25 years, something like a quarter of the workforce in advance societies may be working part or even full-time from home through phone and computer.

From the perspective of employees, a part-time home-office can be close to ideal. They keep the security of their ongoing jobs, but do it more or less unsupervised and in the comfort of home. Several American and European companies have introduced the concept. Employees who are allowed to work partly at home receive a computer and software so their homes can operate as an extension of their offices. And companies believe the arrangement has been worth the investment.

Working at home, free from the constant interruptions of the office, many workers find that it becomes possible to concentrate more deeply on their work and for longer periods of time. More important and creative work is thus being taken home, with routine chores conducted in the office. However, workers like the arrangement where they periodically visit their offices. This keeps them in touch with various developments going on, including office politics.

The practice of permitting part-time work at home looks like it is destined to catch on in the corporate world all over. Corporations have the flexibility and strength to go in for such decentralization; already many firms operate flexible hours. And they can manage the needed technical aids. It is, however, unlikely that something similar will happen in government and other public offices. Of course, we also have the tradition of senior officers taking some files home for study. But this remains a highly informal arrangement, and a good deal dependent on the personal style of functioning of particular officers. Anyway, they still have to be in their office for all the office hours.

With more and more homes as part or full-time offices, homes themselves may undergo a change for the better. "It was just a place to eat, clean and sleep. Now that I work at home several days a week, I take more pride in my environment. I am spending more time making it comfortable," says the owner of a part-time home-office.

When the Wife Outshines

Ravi and Rani have just celebrated their silver wedding anniversary. Ravi had wanted something modest and private; Rani something classy, big and showy. Eventually it went Rani's way.

Bagging a first in MA English literature, Ravi took over as a lecturer in a top Delhi college. Nursed high hopes of professional success, let alone becoming an established writer, probably a novelist.

Tall, handsome, genial, at 27, Ravi was rated a good catch.

Rani held a second-class degree, and a diploma in textile designing. She was not a beauty, but a fairly personable figure who came with a large dowry.

For the first ten years of marriage she busied herself with the household and bringing up two bright boys.

The marital equation clearly favoured Ravi. But by their silver wedding anniversary, the situation stands reversed.

Rani's boutique, opened 15 years back in a rented first-floor attic in Khan Market, has grown into a roaring business. She specializes in women's wear of salwar–kameez. And she has blossomed into an established fashion designer.

By now she has her own impressive premises and showroom in South Extension, backed by a factory in Noida. She employs over fifty people in garment manufacturing. A major part of her production is currently tied to export orders from UK, USA, Canada, Hong Kong, and East/South Africa for the Indian community there.

A happy combination of sustained strenuous work coupled with obsessive concern for detail and perfection, business acumen, and promotional drive has succeeded in making Rani a known figure in the field of fashion designing, ladies' suits. She has built numerous contacts in India and abroad. She travels oversees twice or thrice a year for business, let alone trips to metropolitan cities in the country.

Lately she has authored a book about her clothing designs; a pricey, heavily illustrated coffee-table tome that is selling well, given her near-celebrity status.

Backed by rising income and a heady sense of success, Rani has retained her youngish looks, goes for the best of beauty treatment—including plastic surgery on eyelids, skincare, and classy clothes—and tones up her figure with half an hour of yoga in the morning. She doesn't look more than 33 for her 43 summers.

Ravi had a better start at marriage, but has fallen far behind his outshining wife. A professor, yes, but not even the head of the department; a senior bloke is blocking his promotion. He has written two books, one a critical evaluation of Tennyson's poetry, and another *History of the Indian Novel in English*. It took much pushing to get a publisher. And the books aren't selling; not even the first edition of 500 copies each. For the last two years, Ravi has spent much of his time writing a novel, a story centred on his troubled boyhood. He just finished the first draft of 70,000 words, and his queries have yet to evoke any interest from a reputed publisher. He's passing through a fairly frustrating phase.

Ravi's only consolation, in fact, his pride, is that their two boys are doing brilliantly. The elder is in IIT Delhi and stays in a campus hostel. The younger has just joined Maulana Azad Medical College, and lives with the parents. While the elder one rides an imported BMW motorbike, the younger has a Santro to himself. Both the boys are keen to study further in the USA, and their mother has assured the financial support for it.

Rani's successful business has upped the family's standard of living. They have moved from Ravi's official two-bedroom flat to a bought-out spacious house in Sundar Nagar. Rani goes about in a chauffeured Honda Accord. Ravi is still sticking to his Maruti 800.

What's fascinating is the different ways the two have been reacting to their changing fortunes. When he was up, she seemed genuinely glad for him. Boasted to everyone how well he was doing in his teaching and writing.

Does Ravi return the favour? He, actually, finds ways of countering anything uppity on her part. His negative feelings are particularly noticeable, say at a dinner where she's in the limelight, and he just The Husband. Invited to fashion parties he loses her within seconds. Usually finds himself alone clutching a drink. Dragged into a circle, he could suffer the mortification of watching the light go out of someone's eye when discovered that he wasn't one of the persons who mattered.

He's likely to whisper to Rani as soon as the food finishes: "I'm going home. You can stay on if you want." That's his way of ruining her evening.

And, on reaching the privacy of their home, perhaps he will accuse her of showing off, or boring others with her work. At times, they end up having a row.

Working Women's World

More and more women are now 'working women'. And if their ranks are not swelling that fast, it is not for want of wishing; it is for want of suitable openings and jobs. Our educated urban women—following the example of the West—look toward coming out of domesticity into the field of outside work.

This phenomenon of educated women employed outside their homes in vast numbers spells important changes in society, possibly the most momentous in human history. It will affect us all, men, women and children. Yet what will be the cumulative consequences, only time will tell.

Not everyone welcomes this change in women's roles. Some despair at what they see as the ruination of an arrangement that provided a nice, comfortable home life, with women leading a sheltered existence, children being well-cared for, and of course, the male breadwinners enjoying particular prestige and attention.

Who Works and Why?

In the poor families, women commonly work. But beyond that, the role demarcation was rather clear-cut; man earned, his wife kept home. Some women did pursue vocations or social work yet the basic pattern stayed intact.

Whereas once only the poor and working-class families required two incomes to operate a household, the necessity of two incomes is now cropping up in middle-class urban homes.

The process has been aided by the increasing, almost equal, access of girls to higher education. You see mothers and fathers quite delighted when their daughters acquire education and allied skills. If need be, these daughters can do without total dependence on their husbands. Marriages here are still viewed as lifelong but recognition is drawing that some marriages are liable to run into serious trouble.

Motherhood, once a necessity and a woman's passive destiny, is becoming more a choice. With contraception, women don't have to have babies they don't want. In fact, a lowered birthrate is a necessary condition for women to work outside and gain equality with males.

The key to women's economic emergence is the fact that the educated woman's time has risen in price until it has become, in the eyes of her family members, too valuable to be spent entirely in the home. While the benefits from working for a paid job have been rising, the benefits of staying home are declining, especially for women having fewer children. The social and cultural inhibitions against women working outside their homes, are also wearing thin. In fact, a stage may come some day when you won't really be respected as being a mere housewife. "But what else do you do?" a housewife may be queried.

Of course, in households where the husband has a high income—a successful surgeon or lawyer, a big businessman or a senior executive or someone propertied—most of the wives may still remain at home. The benefit of additional income to such a family is marginal. Again, it is not easy for such wives to obtain work befitting the social status they derive from their husband's position unless a woman is specially qualified, or has a strong inclination to work. Here, another phenomenon is coming into play. Some women work, not because they need the money it brings, but because their work yields them certain satisfaction.

Daughters of working mothers routinely take to work. Another trend is to start an income generating activity at home itself like a coaching class, a boutique, a beauty parlour or some computer work. Husbands like it; they see prospects of additional income without much dislocation to her household work. Unhappily, many of these ventures are known to fold up.

The World of Work

Jobs considered suitable for women are growing rapidly in urban and industrial settings. Clerks were once exclusively male. Gradually, with the entry of women, it is becoming a popular profession for women. Handling cash at banks and shops, once an important male preserve, may soon be changing hands.

The designation of jobs as unsuitable for women is more a matter of convention in a particular society rather than a reflection of women's inherent disabilities and dislikes. In some societies, women do heavy manual work. They are even joining some countries' armed forces in considerable numbers. No doubt prejudices persist against women in professions like, say, staff car drivers with government and companies. An intending female entrant is frightened off, and even women deem it as "unsuitable yet".

Women are again not fully free from a few other discriminations in the world of work, though they have been given the right of equal salary and equal opportunities. In an invidious way, they often get less office information and enjoy less support for entry into higher positions.

Her Home World

Husbands of wives with regular jobs are not seen averaging any significant amounts of extra household work as compared to those with full-time wives, though many of these husbands often admit the need for rendering such help. Some households even expect the same old standard of wifely care and attention. The result: a working wife can be terribly overworked. "It's I who need a 'wife'," one jokingly remarked.

Most present-day males grew up expecting to be waited upon in the home, and to be exempt from any share in cooking, cleaning and upkeep of clothes. It can be very difficult for a wife to prevail upon her husband to do anything he dislikes to do—and men dislike doing a host of "unmanly" things. He may refuse her request outright or simply ignore the suggestions. Or he may say he'll do it but fail to do so or do it badly on purpose or discontinue doing it after a while. Too many reminders from her will be construed as nagging, and despoil the marriage itself. Many wives give up the attempt, and seek relief through hiring extra help. The latter course finds more favour with the husbands. In fact, husbands are the principal beneficiaries of working wives. They come into double incomes without any appreciable addition to their work—at the most a little inconvenience at times.

Luckily for us, house help is still available. Again, a working wife may have the assistance of a live-in relative, though such help is often not without its own complications. By and large, a working wife has very little leisure time for resting or attending to her personal needs. She is usually working when other members of the family are watching TV or reading papers or otherwise enjoying themselves.

One saving grace: housework is, to an extent, a variable commodity. You can cut down a good deal on cleaning and general upkeep without doing serious injury to the quality of life. And working wives simply do housework faster. They usually develop the knack of doing more than one thing at a time, as well as coordinating the activities better.

The inevitable trend of educated women coming into the world of work in large numbers would herald fundamental changes in our social and economic life. New norms of family living and marital equations have to be evolved. The changes will invoke many painful adjustments and reorientation of attitudes. But one can be buoyed with the belief that human beings are ingenious enough to meet such challenges.

Men and Women at Work

Are men and women the same at work?

To feminists, a perfect gender balance is achievable in all occupations. Many psychologists think otherwise.

Feminists themselves continue to be divided into minimizers and maximizers of the male–female differences. The issue actually confronts them with an awkward ideological dilemma. If men and women are basically the same, the feminist goal becomes equality; that also restrains them from attacking men or celebrating women. If the two are inherently different, feminists can point with pride to women's special attributes—but then the concept of equality takes a backseat.

Psychologists rely on a wealth of accumulating evidence that shows men and women having different intellectual aptitudes. Men excel in mathematical and scientific pursuits; women have an edge in language skills. School examination results amply bear out the same.

The differences in ability are now known to result from differences in brain structure as influenced by hormones during prenatal development. The most striking difference is that male brains are more specialized in spatial processing in the right hemisphere. Female brains appear better equipped for communication between the two hemispheres. One result: male brains are more susceptible to damage as they have no back-up if something goes wrong in one hemisphere, hence are more prone to disorders such as stammering or dyslexia.

Women are surely moving into many fields of work that were once male preserves. Their performance should be no different from men in occupations that were male preserves from arbitrary convention or vested power (office work, administration). But performance differential isn't likely to be eliminated totally in occupations that have a biological foundation (scientific research, engineering).

Another major difference between typical men and women that has relevance to work pertains to personality traits, such as competitiveness and ambitiousness. Men are typically more motivated than women in pursuit of status and economic rewards, whatever occupation they choose. And this tendency of males to be more competitive than women has been observed as common to almost all societies in the world, thus confirming its probable biological origins.

No wonder most judges, bank managers, company directors, and top doctors are men, though women have been coming into medicine, law, finance, judiciary and even business. Some element of male discrimination may be there, and men admittedly had a head start, yet men's higher competitiveness may be the crucial factor.

Here, the role of evolutionary psychology would be hard to ignore. During evolution, high male status must have expanded sexual access to females, as it does in many species of animals. Given this distinctly male link between social achievement and genetic proliferation, it is plausible to assume that millions of years of evolution would endow males with a distinctive thirst for power. In almost all human societies, the average male is seen pursuing status and power more fiercely and opportunistically than his female counterpart.

Not only does prenatal testosterone causes competitive aggressiveness, but the experience of triumph releases further testosterone. Thus, a sharp elevation in status, even a victory in sports, operates as an aphrodisiac, while failure or defeat changes a male's brain chemicals towards those seen in depressed patients. Female sexual responsiveness, by contrast, is said to be actually enhanced by the sense of being overpowered. Anyway, success in life does not boost female sexuality; the same possibly diminishes it.

Women, however, enjoy an advantage in work involving social situations. They are far better than men at reading non-verbal signals of emotion—what's called body language. And they are more alert at assessing the significance of small details. This superior social perceptiveness is commonly referred to as female intuition. The experience of dealing with the needs and wiles of young children may also be equipping women particularly well as better negotiators. Women clearly show greater understanding of other people and this is a valuable asset in many professions, such as teaching, nursing, counseling—even in areas like real estate and insurance.

If women lack aggressiveness in the sales field, they evidently make up for it with other advantages, such as verbal fluency and the management of social situations. Men are more likely to evoke resistance by adopting the hard-sell approach.

In short, men and women are quite different at work, and these differences are largely innate. Men are almost certain to predominate in many occupations while women enjoy significant advantages in certain callings. To that extent, the two complement each other rather than oppose.

3

Sex in Marriage

Matters of Marital Sex

Few fields of human activity happen to be attracting as much advice as marital sex. Here is some more on the same subject, apparently an inexhaustible subject.

A wife getting up to wash immediately after sex may well be sending a wrong signal. The husband is likely to interpret it as his wife's desire to literally wash him away. Jumping up after sex does convey a message of distaste, thus dampening the afterglow.

One simple solution is to keep a towel or some tissues by the bed. It's worth postponing your cleanup if it means preserving the intimacy between you and your husband. Anyway, make sure he understands that you never intended to hurt him; you just wanted to avoid the drippy discomfort.

The syndrome of Inhibited Sex Drive (ISD) is known to mar many a marriage. A partner suffering from ISD can take to avoiding sex. A standard tactic is to go to bed long before your spouse does, so that you will be asleep, or can feign sleep, when the partner joins up. Or, in reverse, a wife disinclined to sex may linger on inordinately over her household chores. The ardour of the waiting husband usually cools off in the process.

Of course, even the most loving couples occasionally experience dry spells—the desire disappearing altogether for days or weeks through crisis or stress or overwork. This phenomenon particularly surfaces up with today's career-oriented couples. However, such phases pass away, more so when the couple take a vacation together. No wonder, frequent vacations of short duration are coming into vogue, instead of the traditional annual one.

Yet ISD is a more worrying matter. In one of its variations, a person is put off all sex by some hormonal imbalance, or deep-seated depression, or emotional conflicts. In the other, a more common form of ISD, you continue to harbour sexual fantasies and longings with respect to some other partners, but cease to feel sexy towards your own spouse.

In fact, without realizing that you are doing so, you may be engaging in negative feelings or "anti-fantasies" about your spouse. A husband may picture his wife to be sloppy or her voice disagreeably squeaky, or having the knack of bringing up unpleasant issues during sex. A wife imagining her hubby to be sweaty or uncouth, or has come to hate his beery breath. Feelings of anger or disappointment towards one's mate play havoc with sexual desire. Once such negative feelings come to be nursed, your sexual appetite for your spouse plummets dramatically.

A good strategy in sex is to focus on the pleasant attributes of one's spouse; things like his muscular chest or her beautiful feet. Couples should be able to discuss their ISD problem in a calm, loving manner. If this does not work, then perhaps they should consult a professional sex therapist.

Marital Sex: Use It or Lose It

That's the phrase making the rounds these days, as if sexual activity was like any other physical workout. "The less sex you have, the less you want," say the experts.

But too much emphasis on frequency of marital sex can also hurt a relationship. Why should a couple who average lovemaking once a fortnight and are content with it, start worrying because surveys have shown other couples making love twice a week? Again you don't have to compete with the sort of love life depicted in some paperback novels; the latter rarely reflect reality.

However, if you do feel that your marital sex is sluggish, there are ways of pepping it up. Sexual experimentation is one. The reason why some couples can experiment sexually is that they know failures won't make them look foolish. They have learned to laugh at flops.

Partners who enjoy good sex don't let their bodies go. They take care of their health, watch their weight, and maintain high standards of personal hygiene and grooming. They keep their bodies clean, hair neat and nails trimmed. Teeth are brushed before getting into bed. They sport attractive nightclothes, and their bedroom is a private, pleasant place. One mother of a four and a six-year old encourages her kids to manage their own breakfast on Sunday mornings so she and her husband can linger on in bed and then take a shower together.

And loving couples never withhold sex to get back at each other for real or imagined grievances.

Women's Orgasm

Of late, perhaps too much has been talked about or written on this subject. Apparently nature has shortchanged women. While healthy men climax like clockwork during intercourse, the majority of women do not, or at least were not doing so till recent times.

An American psychotherapist, Edward W. Eichel, encourages couples in adopting a method of intercourse that is a variation of the missionary position. It not only increases the chances of coital orgasm, it even tends to bring on that rarest of ecstasies—simultaneous orgasm. Eichel's study of forty-three of the men and women who tested the method was published in the prestigious *Journal of Sex and Marital Therapy*.

The main idea is to manage thrusts that give continuous stimulation to the clitoris. The vaginal thrusts alone can't do the trick; vaginal walls have almost no nerve endings.

Incidentally, we who gave the *Kamasutra* to the world don't seem to have a specific word for female orgasm. The Japanese word for it translates like, "I have died and gone to heaven".

Excuses, Excuses

Recently, a neurology professor at Southern Illinois University reports that sex is one of the best cures for relieving a headache. Especially if the sex takes place within the first thirty minutes after the onset of the headache.

Thus, the most acceptable excuse known to mankind regarding not to have sex now bites the dust. Instead of "Not tonight, I've a headache", we may now be hearing, "Hurry up, I've a headache".

Women who "aren't in the mood" will have to coin new excuses; things like "it's too late", or "the kids will hear", or "my nails are wet", or "we just did it last week". Faking a headache wouldn't be enough.

And what excuse does a hubby trot out if for the moment he finds himself under the weather.

Spicing Marital Sex: Go Beyond 50/50

Many modern couples have come to believe that sexual intimacy between spouses is best attained through a 50/50 ideal of equality. But then some of them are discovering to their dismay that equality, by itself, is not making for a passionate relationship.

Wives commonly complain that their men are behaving less sexy, seemingly lost in their work life. Women often ask why men are such "wimps" these days.

Husbands complain that wives are becoming hardened, more resistive, and independent to the point that they no longer attract, sexually. In short, men often ask why women are becoming such "ball-breakers" these days.

So, Where Do We Get from Here?

Esther Perel, a noted American psychotherapist, writing in *Psychotherapy Networker* (May/June 2003), however, makes out that belief in equality, consensus-building, fairness and tolerance (very desirable features otherwise in marriage or elsewhere) can, in the bedroom, result in very boring sex. Sexual excitement often thrives on power plays, role reversals, imperious demand, and seductive manipulations. It's the complementarity—the appeal of difference—rather than strict gender equality that makes couples more erotic.

Couples, she say, should recover their curiosity, hone their senses to see the invisible and hear the inaudible.

Joy of Sex

The doctor who propagated inventive, carefree and joyous sex has passed away at the age of eighty.

Today's sexual scene is vastly different from that of the early 1970s when Alex Comfort wrote an inhibition-breaking book *The Joy of Sex.* Yet his rather refreshing approach to sex as something unanxious and playful did contribute in no small measure to moulding prevailing mores about lovemaking and sex.

The Joy of Sex—dubbed by some as the *Kamasutra* brought up to date— turned out to be a smashing hit, a record-breaking international bestseller. It was everywhere, in bookshops, in homes, even in libraries. While many read it openly, a lot more read it surreptitiously. And to many others the most enticing part of the book was its illustrations; explicit photographs and drawings of a naked young couple—a man with a bushy beard and a woman with bushy armpits—in umpteen forms of lovemaking. It was said that at one time the two books most stolen were the Bible and *The Joy of Sex.*

Dr. Comfort's (the name itself no less appropriate) fame now rests entirely on this 'sex manual'—originally intended as a text for medical students.

Presumably many of us have read *The Joy of Sex.* But if you haven't, the book can come as an interesting read, though it was written nearly 40 years back.

The Joy of Sex or *A Gourmet Guide to Lovemaking* is structured like a cookery book: Starters, Main Courses, Sauces and Pickles. Starters deal with things such as beds, deodorants, body parts (especially genitals), and the appeal of nakedness. The main dish is loving, unselfconscious intercourse—long, frequent, varied, ending with both parties satisfied. Sauces and pickles speak of a few sexual deviations and the use of various objects for sexual titillation. To Comfort, there are only two "rules" in good sex: One is "Don't do anything you don't really enjoy", and the other is "Find out your partner's needs and don't balk them if you can help it".

He has some suggestions for long-term loving couples on how to get the best out of the book. "Read through or dip into this book together and separately. These are all techniques which straight people need and use to fill out their sex lives, or simply enjoy as play and relaxation. . . . Go by your own needs and your partner's. Do note anything, which turns one or both of you on to the point of saying "I'd like to try that". If you are shy of talking about sexual needs, make a list of page numbers you'd like your partner to read, and exchange lists. Then take it mutually from there. You will find out things about each other you didn't know, and all of them will be rewarding."

Now this is not any obsolescent advice: many of today's couples stay shy of signaling to each other their sexual needs, urges, or arousals. Anything that could help them overcome this awkwardness should be welcome. "The aim of *The Joy of Sex* is to stimulate your creative imagination," says Comfort.

Hundreds of books on sex counselling have come out since *The Joy of Sex*. Of late particularly, there's a rash of "straight books" and "counselling" magazines. Yet none has been able to rival Comfort's book in style, substance and popularity. He still carries the title, the "Doctor of Love," or "Dr. Sex."

Sex Life of Dual-Career Couples

Pran and Poonam are a career-couple in their late thirties, he a leading lawyer, she heading a noted travel agency.

They have everything one commonly wants: money, health, work satisfaction, a loving relationship, and two nice kids, a girl of ten and a boy of seven. Yet sometimes a whole month passes without an episode of sex between them.

Pran and Poonam may well be relieved to learn that, even in the most stellar dual-career marriages, months can go by without "action". Almost everything in the contemporary dual-career couple's life operates against marital sex. No wonder this group of people has earned the acronym DINS—double income, no sex. It's essentially a lifestyle problem, not a sexual problem.

Some career-couples make a laugh of their "pathetic" sex life—no spunk remaining to invest in it after the exhausting demands of work life. Many professional women admit to having hardly anything left over at the end of the day after working aggressively all day in what is largely a man's world. On top of that, so many careers these days involve a lot of travelling.

Pran starts his workday around seven in the morning, labouring over his briefs. He starts seeing clients by 8. After a full day at the courts, he's again at his home office till nearly 9, preparing briefs and talking to his clients. "It's work, work, all the time. I've let my physical, sensual side go, and when you do that your sex drive just shrivels up. And then you start fearing your own performance and so avoid sex," he confides.

After a quick bath, a large whisky, dinner and a little rap with kids, it's time for the 10.30 pm BBC news. "Give a man the option of watching late news or having sex with his mate, and he'll almost always choose the former," says a wit.

Poonam's work hours—9 to 6—are relatively shorter. But then she keeps receiving oversees calls at all odd hours. And has to undertake a hectic travel schedule. Over and above this, there is the unending business of running an elaborate household, the upkeep of her wardrobe, and finding what's called 'quality time' for kids.

Only on rare occasions are the two partners free at the same time, and suitably relaxed for sex. Women, sexologists say, usually need to feel relaxed before they are in a mood for sex, while men often need to have sex before they can feel relaxed. This quirk of nature can exacerbate the "Not now" syndrome in an already complex sex situation obtaining within a career-couple.

And quite a few hurdles go like this:

Does she have to get up early for work?

Has he to catch an early morning flight to a city for a case?

Is any family member in the midst of a crisis?

Any significant aches or pains she had in the last thirty minutes?

As children enter the picture, sex takes a back seat for some time—many parents going into a sexual hiatus that could last a year with every childbirth. Parental fatigue mounts up. In our Indian conditions, the presence of servants or some live-in relative does help but then these generate their own problems. The demands of kids, coupled with all the other pressures of life, don't exactly turn a career woman into a sex kitten.

And when kids grow up—these days they hang around into adulthood, some refusing to leave home altogether—privacy is a big factor. You feel the way you used to feel trying to do 'it' at other people's houses.

What keeps most career couples going through the dry spells is that they pay much attention to connecting on a daily basis. Touching each other now and then is a common tactic, even if no sex is wanted. "I can't imagine not being entwined in his arms when we start sleeping," says one woman. "I can't imagine going without the day-to-day physicality, the hugs, the kisses, the emotional intimacy. It is this consistency that's comforting." Anyway, couples mostly tend to make no big deal about the frequency of sex, if the relationship is otherwise cruising along nicely.

Two-career couples, say some experts, may have to fall back on appointment-book sex if their sex lives are going out of whack. Where a couple finds that sex is getting pushed off the schedule by other commitments, it's time to get out their appointment books and mark each other in, better with indelible ink. Setting aside, say, every week, a block of time—two to three hours—for each other, to crawl into bed and cuddle. Occasionally this could be afternoons; the time men are known to get more horny.

Again, the levels of testosterone in men and progesterone in women are significantly higher in the morning hours than at any other time. That way, the best time for lovemaking may well be morning.

A couple is advised to keep its appointments with each other. Don't let fatigue or other put-offs (guests in the house, an unexpected engagement, a particular TV programme or sports fixture) keep you from this primary tryst. Every put-off is a put-down. It sends a signal you don't deem your partner as important as some other activity.

The video revolution has been a blessing for many couples confronting the problems of flagging desire. Couples have been reporting a far livelier love scene as they watched an erotic film together. Admittedly, for a majority of women porn is still a problem but, of late, the porn industry has been cleaning up its act to attract women viewers.

What possibly produces the best results is a respite; both from home and work. No wonder long-weekend trips or short holiday excursions are the in-thing these days. If you can manage one—possibly dumping your small kids with their grandparents—nothing equals a nice holiday for boosting a couple's sex life. Better still if you keep your cellular phones deactivated for most of the holiday time.

Sexual Liveliness in Long Marriages

"We've had an active sex life for over forty years. Of course, it is not the same as what it was in the beginning. It's more affectionate and friendly than passionate these days, and nowhere as frequent, but a great source of love and comfort to both of us." —A man of 65

Is sex in long relationships really as bad as it's joked about? Obviously, it is for some couples. There is a lot of dysfunctional, unsatisfying sex in many marriages. One reason, of course, is that most of these marriages themselves leave a lot to be desired.

The main argument against good sex in the long run is what's called the Coolidge Effect, based on a story about the American President Calvin Coolidge. The president and his wife had been given separate tours while visiting a poultry farm. Mrs. Coolidge saw a rooster mounting a hen and asked how often this happened. The answer was many times each day. “Please tell that to the President,” she said. When the president was informed of the rooster’s performance, he inquired whether it was with the same hen. “Oh, no,” was the answer, “a different one each time.” “Tell that to Mrs. Coolidge,” replied the president.

No doubt, fresh flesh turns us on, especially men. And it’s usually the man who determines how much sex there is in a marriage.

A number of surveys, however, strongly suggest that married men and women have more and better sex than anyone else. If we look at subjective satisfaction, studies indicate that both men and women are more satisfied with marital sex than with outside flings.

What keeps the sex spark alive in a long relationship?

Experts have a few explanations to offer as well as some words of advice.

One way to have better sex life over time with the same partner is to do whatever is necessary to combat the taking-her-for-granted syndrome. Admittedly, the thrill of the chase is not there; you can have her when you want. Yet men are advised to bring an element of courting to enliven the proceedings.

Couples managing good sex over time put sex high on the list of priorities. They are willing to do what it takes to find time for it. It could mean arranging vacations just for the two of them, without children or friends. It could mean turning down the requests of relatives to stay at their place for extended periods. It may also mean that you keep track of how often good sex is happening.

Good sex flourishes only when there is time for it. In many marriages the partners spend little quality time together. When they are together, they’re mostly dealing with money matters, children, and other household work. When they go out, they often go with others. They spend little time together, free of distractions.

A majority of couples, when questioned, make out that they had more and better sex on vacations than at other times. So one way to keep sex lively in a marriage is to plan numerous vacations, at least some of them just for the two of them.

Timing means two things, seemingly contradictory things. First is that you plan for being together and for sex. Second is that you seize the times that come up spontaneously. Couples enjoying good sex are known to take advantage of both.

One characteristic of satisfied couples is that although they disagree and argue and have periods when they can't talk to each other, as do all couples, they recover quickly. They tend not to sulk or carry around anger for long periods. Emotional distance at midlife can increase sexual distance, when you and your partner misinterpret each other's actions and intentions.

Midlife change comes in many forms, some of which can affect you sexually, such as financial anxiety, problems with adolescent or adult children, or ageing parents who suddenly need help.

People who have good sex over time tend to be sensual. They understand the importance of hand-holding, hugs, kisses or just touching for touching sake. And this touching is not done in a perfunctory manner. It is unhurried, gentle touching that conveys love and closeness. Women routinely complain that men are too hurried and too rough in touching. Not that a quick, firm touch is not appropriate at times, but mostly it needs to be soft and slow.

Sexy couples believe in romancing. They know the importance of surprise, tenderness, compliments, and all those special little things. They comment on how sexy or lovely the partner looks; they occasionally arrange romantic dinners; they remember special days and come up with surprise presents.

And couples who have good sex over the years learn to play at it rather than work at it. They have fun with it.

Playing at sex also means not having any rigid rules about it, being tolerant of what it is and what it can give. This is especially important for older people, with age and illness taking a toll. These couples do not go into hysterical overdrive when they aren't functioning perfectly but instead they use what they have to enjoy themselves.

It is important to remind your partner periodically of what you need, such as more foreplay. Just because you told your partner several years ago, doesn't mean he'll remember. In fact, if it's physically important to you but not to him, it's normal for him to forget.

Tell your partner what feels good and what doesn't. Be positive, but don't hesitate to guide your partner's hand when necessary.

Children are hazardous to good sex unless you are aware of the difficulties and prepared to deal with them. Parents who have good sex have found it necessary to carve out and protect private time for themselves. They make it clear from the outset that, barring emergencies, there are times when they are not to be disturbed. One couple was putting up a "Do Not Disturb" sign. It meant that their three kids were not to knock on the door, make loud noises near it, or get into fights when the sign was up.

The Changing Pattern of Pornography

Pornography may be changing; some say, changing for the better. Not that pornographers have suffered a change of heart. Or not that their male clients have been put off the "dirty" stuff. Pornography may be changing because more and more women are joining in as home viewers of porn videos.

This entry of women as porn viewers can be attributed more to technology than to a change in their attitudes. It is the technology of video cassettes and the Internet that has brought film viewing into the privacy and comfort of one's home and at the timings of one's choice.

Modern video cameras wielded by amateurs may be heralding another change. Couples can make home movies of their own. Sex at 10, film at 11.

Throughout its long history, pornography—an instrument of sexual arousal—has been shaped by technology. It was mainly expressed in jokes and riddles, ribald verses and stories, till printing was invented. A book was a handy object to handle. And the clandestine circulation of books was not hard to manage.

Pornography underwent another change with the coming of photography and the motion picture. The era of pictorial porn magazine and porn films was ushered in. Rapid advances in photography, colour and image projection helped make pornographic material sexually more explicit—more arousing as well as more offensive.

The word pornography is from the Greek porno (prostitute) and graphien (to write), thus any literature depicting the life of prostitutes. In a way the word is getting inappropriate for present day pornography, which hardly figures in written form.

Pornography has taken the most dramatic turn with the coming of video cassettes and the Internet. People don't have to queue up for X-rated films or trek to "adult movies" centres. Patrons don't have to haunt sleazy places for seeing porn films or run the risks of encountering shady characters while out watching such stuff. They can now simply take CDs or video cassettes home if they have the equipment. In some countries, even cable TV has pitched in by providing a soft-porn subscriber channel, like the Playboy Channel.

The cassette player has put porn where it belongs: in people's bedrooms. Some couples may be using it as a regular prelude to sex. "People feel that in the comfort of their homes they are allowed to be a little more wicked."

The phenomenon of wives watching porn along with their husbands has strong implications for the porn industry. It has to have its products cleaned up a bit. At least the semblance of a story and some pursuit of it before the clothes come off. Impatient males watching alongside have to put up with some minutes of story development before the "action" starts.

Producers of pornographic films are trying to inject romance and feelings in their shows so that the traditional female repugnance to porn could be melted. The scenes have to be placed in more glamorous settings than a mere bed in a room. And a cast of better acting ability brought in. Often a dash of humour is added to enliven the proceedings. The industry feels confident that women can be lured to soft porn if the product is wrapped inside a pleasing story and does not show women in degrading positions.

The TV Hug

William Cane has written a book *The Art of Hugging* (St Martin's Press). Cane is already the author of a book *The Art of Kissing.*

In his latest one on hugging, the writer provides instructions for more than twenty-five different hugs, including the long hug, the platonic hug, and the comforting hug.

Here are a few of the points made out by him in the chapter on "The Television Hug".

When they are at home, 62 percent of American men and women enjoy television hugs more than just about any other kind. "We like to sit side by side on the love seat, sometimes with my arm around her or hers around me. Or we watch a show lying on the couch, with her in front of me," says a husband.

Women sometimes like you to stroke their hair and groom them during the television hug. Another thing a woman likes is to sit on your lap. She'll appreciate if you allow her to do so without interruption. This doesn't mean you have to let her cut off your circulation. Make it easy on yourself and take a break during commercials to stretch your legs.

Sometimes a woman is happy just to be able to lean against you while you're watching television. Tell her to rest her head on your shoulder. Stroke her hair now and then. Snake an arm around if you can. Or place your hand on her knee or thigh.

Men like it when women spoon with them on the couch while watching television. This usually involves the two of you lying on your sides close together, like a couple of spoons, both of you facing the television so that you can see the show.

"When we watch TV, I generally spoon with her in front, my arm draped over her, and her legs intertwined with mine," says another husband.

The most important thing to remember about the television hug is to stay focused on your partner's needs. One woman says she gets annoyed when hugging her mate if he gets too engrossed in the programme and seems less interested in the hugging.

Infidelity

In an age of greater sexual freedom, couples seem to be getting more intolerant of infidelity. That's the irony and paradox. Fidelity actually rates as a top priority with most couples in these days of increasing sexual liberation.

People may have had a range of sexual experiences before marriage—penalty for that is on the decline—but modern marriage has come to expect exclusivity, along with a good sexual relationship. This is partly a consequence of women's advancing equality in economic and social spheres.

The strong antipathy to infidelity poses its dangers too. It is surmised (admission about affairs is hard to come by, even under terms of anonymity) that a majority of men and a sizeable minority of women have at least one extramarital affair. Men seem to do it out of curiosity; women in their search for intimacy. Perhaps a part of the fascination lies in doing something forbidden, taking a risk, stepping outside permitted boundaries.

Types of Infidelity

Admittedly each affair is unique in its start and development, its love and pain, its attraction and conflict. Yet affairs can be grouped into three broad categories: accidental infidelity, romantic infidelity, and philandering. The bulk of first affairs is of the accidental type, unintended, almost acts of carelessness. And the most accident-prone are men who drink hard, travel a lot, and have buddies who screw around.

An accidental affair is apt to produce a typical response in the guilty party. Either one feels remorse and resolves to be more careful in future—confessing it to one's mate is a rarity. Or, blame it on the frigidity of one's married partner or on some other imagined grievance.

Romantic infidelity—falling in love with someone—is much more destructive of marriage. You imagine you've met somebody wonderful, somebody who'll transform your life for the better. The fact that wonderful people don't usually mess around with married ones gets obscured.

To a person undergoing a phase of depression or otherwise facing a life crisis, an affair with someone decades younger or older, someone dependent or dominating, can prove quite stimulating. The depression is often lifted, though it is likely to recur, and with greater intensity as alienation builds up with one's married partner.

Both men and women are quite capable of sliding into this temporary insanity. However men in love can be unbelievably incautious and willing to give up everything. Men in love lose their heads—at least for a while. Romantic affairs lead to a great many divorces, separations, even suicides.

There are others who continue with their marriage—a marriage that won't die and won't revive—by recourse to keeping a mistress or a boyfriend. In such a regular arrangement outside marriage, the intensity of romance doesn't stay at a fever pitch; it stabilizes at a lower level.

Philandering is a predominantly male activity. Philanderers take up infidelity as a hobby, a recreation. Whether sex addicts or not, these men use sex compulsively to affirm their masculinity—to them their most valuable attribute. Their life is centred around trying to impress women with their physical strength, seductive skills, power, wealth, and, if necessary, force. Some of them are quite charming and become adept in finding women eager to be abused by them.

They think they are normal men, that they are doing what every other real man would do if he weren't such a wimp.

Men are able to approach extra-marital sex more casually than women. It's not only the patriarchal double standard but, as one wit said, the difference between having genitals on the outside and having them inside.

There are female philanderers too. Mentally, they say, every single married woman has extra-marital fantasies about other men at some time or another. However, actual philanderers are found more often among single or divorced women; straying wives are rarely philanderers. Female philanderers prefer to raid other people's marriages. Some of them who pursue married men solely to restore their own sense of power are known as "spider women".

Factors Favouring Infidelity in Women

1. Opportunity is one of the prime reasons that an affair takes place. Virtue is not the only reason for fidelity; lack of opportunity is often a factor.
2. Work outside the home. Some link between employment and infidelity has been identified. A majority of employed unfaithful wives are known to have met their lovers through work.
3. An intimate friendship with a man. Gradually it gets them more emotionally involved. If the relationship continues, it can very often lead to sex—from friends into lovers.
4. Surveys have shown that women who are better educated than their husbands have significantly higher rates of infidelity than those lesser educated.
5. A link between sex before marriage and extramarital sex; the more of the first, the greater the likelihood of the second.
6. A crisis point in life—the death of a parent, stress of moving to a strange place, or even a birth or illness—can make a woman more prone to an extramarital affair.

Myths About Infidelity

1. *Everybody is unfaithful; it's expected behaviour.* Conceivably there's a lot of infidelity around; still most people are faithful most of the time. Without the expectation of fidelity, marriage will lose much of its meaning.
2. *Affairs are good for you; an affair may even revive a dull marriage.* Whatever the theorists may say, the reality is

that infidelity, whether it is furtive or blatant, eventually does no good to a marriage. Indeed, the same can ruin it.

3. *People have affairs because they are oversexed.* Most affairs consist of less sex and more planning, less of bed and more of telephoning. In general, monogamous couples have a lot more satisfying sex than the people who are screwing around.
4. *People have affairs because they aren't in love with their marriage partners.* Often it turns out that a marriage was fine before the affair happened; the lack of love in marriage is more of an afterthought to justify the affair. Anyway, being in love with one's mate does not protect a person from lust.

Many an infidel adopts the strategy of denying the affair with the utmost vehemence and persistence, despite clear indications to the contrary. Once an affair is known or even strongly suspected, there is no safety in denial, but there is hope in admission. In fact, the continued lying and denial is the more unforgivable aspect of the infidelity.

It cannot be denied that some of the most transforming and positive love affairs have been adulterous. Yet it can be easily made out that in normal, everyday marriages, an affair is not a safe treatment for depression, boredom, or an imperfect marriage.

Speaking of Adultery ...

- Most women believe that if the partners love each other, they won't be interested in an affair. And this is commonly true of women. A wife's infidelity is often a consequence of her continuing unhappiness with marriage. Gradually she begins to withdraw from her mate. And in her loneliness, she becomes emotionally available for an affair. It is then a question of her being taken in by someone interesting and the opportunities for dalliance.
- Men's behaviour works out different. Many happily-married men who love their partner and enjoy good sex at home don't turn down an opportunity for extramarital sex. It's not a question of not getting enough sex at home, but of variety and the adrenaline surge of a new conquest. For

many men such extramarital sex holds slight or no emotional involvement; it's plain physical sex. The phenomenon is rather baffling to women who tend to consider sex as an offshoot of emotional involvement.

- Another myth is the hydraulic pump theory—that you only have limited energy for something. If the man was having sex outside, he wouldn't be wanting that much at home, and his wife would get to know of it. Actually some men become more passionate at home when having extramarital sex; they are sexually roused by the affair. Women, on the contrary, often develop disinterest in marital sex when having an affair.
- Technology is having its own impact on affairs. Now you have cyber affairs. Clandestine meetings are again easier to fix up, aided by cell phones, the Internet and e-mail. But then quite a few people have discovered a partner's affair by getting the cellular phone bill listing the numbers dialed. Or taking the partner's beeper and seeing who has been calling. We are leaving a whole new electronic trail.
- To catch their cheating husbands, Japanese women are said to be seeking the aid of forensic science. Using chemicals anyway works out cheaper than the old-fashioned method of hiring a detective to tail a straying husband. One detective technique employs two chemicals supplied in aerosol cans. Each of these is spread on the suspect underwear in turn. If traces of seminal fluid are present—these can be detected for hours or days later on if the underwear remains unwashed—the second spray turns the seminal spots bright green. It's the same test employed in forensic labs to detect presence of semen in criminal cases.
- Men have often sought justification for their philandering on the "frugality" and "restrictiveness" of the home fare.
- What is the psyche of wives who seek love outside marriage or succumb to it? Normally, many a married woman has extra-marital fantasies about other men at some time or another. But why do stably married women embroil themselves in actual affairs? It could be a weakness for excitement or the effect of sustained flattery or the lure

of expensive gifts and entertainment. It could be the vulnerability of someone whose husband was mostly away. Or a married woman finding someone with whom she wants to forge a permanent relationship, to the detriment of her marriage.

Addicted to Sex

For twenty years, right since he turned fourteen, sex has dominated Satish's life. Starting with sexual escapades with a live-in cousin, his whole life seems to have narrowed down to a frenzied search for sexual encounters and thrills.

"I am incapable of having a conversation with a woman without making sexual overtures," he admits. "Even after marriage, I'm always mentally having sex with other women I see in shops or social gatherings."

And Satish does succeed in making a few conquests. However, having a horror of being involved in any sex scandal, he mostly opted for prostitutes. Indeed, he had perfected a drill for such forays. Fortified with a couple of drinks, he went for the quick, protected by a condom. Often, he kept his shoes on. Hardly any words exchanged beyond the initial bargaining. And he would stay quite oblivious to the grimy surroundings.

Now for the last few years he has cut down on prostitutes for fear of AIDS and the other hassles involved. Instead, he has been concentrating more on servant maids, cleaning women, and others of lower orders.

Satish continues to be an avid consumer of pornography. He buys copies of *Hustler* when he goes abroad and also porn films. Of late he has started surfing porn on the Internet in the privacy of his study.

Happily he has been able to keep under control dangerous sexual urges such as exhibitionism or child molestation (though he's developing a morbid interest in girls of 9–10). But he's grown into an almost compulsive voyeur. Exposed female bodies fascinate him to no end. Given a chance, he spends hours on topless Mediterranean beaches. And a recent trip to a nudist beach in Germany drove him nearly crazy with excitement.

Satish is a senior executive in a multinational firm. Yet he can't help harbouring a guilty feeling that a more successful career eluded him because so much of his time and attention was drained away chasing promiscuous sex or fantasizing about it.

"Am I oversexed?" he often asks himself. There is no meter for such things. And sex isn't like alcohol where consumption beyond a point categorizes you as alcoholic. There isn't a cutoff point for sexual activity. Maybe, many other people were sexually as active as he. "Everyone without exception enjoys a sexual life far more active and more rewarding than can be guessed at even by his close friends," says Brendan Gill.

At times Satish wonders what went wrong with him? Is it simply a case of self-indulgence or a lack of scruples? Or does it stem from causes beyond his control, such as genes? Psychiatrists say that a majority of sex addicts (the term used for want of a better word) are raised in dysfunctional families or they had been sexually abused as children. His childhood was no different from that of his three brothers and they aren't sexaholics (as far as he can make out). At eleven he had been sexually assaulted by the trusted family servant but then his brothers might have been through a similar experience.

There is the other view that compulsive sexual behaviour is rooted in low self-esteem, where every sexual conquest becomes an ego trip. But he wasn't particularly lacking in self-esteem. He had done well in studies and sports. Landed a good job. Now he's married to a presentable dental surgeon and is the father of a bright kid.

Experts estimate that 7 to 10 per cent of the world's adults could be engaged in compulsive sexual behaviour of some kind; the incidents are far more than is commonly thought. Sexaholics are said to figure in every society and in every country. And by no means are they all men—there are women sexaholics, too.

4

Money in Marriage

Meaning of Money

The word "money" comes from the Latin word *moneta*. Roman coins were first struck at the temple of the goddess Juno Moneta. She was worshipped for her wise counsel—somewhat akin to our goddess Lakshmi.

Yet many people lose their judgment and discrimination when it comes to matters of money. Each of us seems to be endowed with a money complex—an intertwined group of psychological "weak spots" that, in various circumstances, erupt into seemingly irrational behaviour.

Marrying partners bring extensive monetary histories with their marriage, just as they bring complex sexual pasts. A breach of fiscal trust or financial 'infidelity' can be as destabilizing of marriage as a sexual affair.

Our money attitudes are not isolated phenomenon but an integral part of what we are. Someone who is withholding money may also be withholding affection. Another one who is perennially anxious about financial status may be lacking in self-assurance. Someone who is ever impoverishing himself financially is harbouring self-destructive behaviour.

Money's meaning differs from person to person, the way beauty differs in the eye of the beholder. Money may be experienced as a weapon or shield, a sedative or a stimulant, a talisman or an aphrodisiac. Having money may bring on feelings of fullness, pride, even sexual attractiveness.

The rising consumer culture and globalization have given rise to an almost obsessive concern with money. People are judged by the cars they keep, the houses they live in, the gadgets they use, the holidays they take, and the healthcare services they employ. We have come to believe that we are entitled to what those who we associate with have.

Professional success and status have their importance but what currently matters most is the acquisition of money. With the steady decline in other forms of distinctions, money is now the chief maker and marker of status and power. As such, the ability to spend and borrow money impulsively has never been greater.

Matters of Money

Many a partner at marriage, particularly the groom, may be burdened with a debt, thus bringing what is termed "the negative dowry". Or the spouse may have less income than has been made out. This produces an evident strain on a new marriage.

Commonly, couples happen to be polarized over money matters. If one is a spender, the other is a hoarder. If one is a worrier about money, the other tends to overlook financial problems. A husband not believing in spending much money on gifts to family and friends is usually mated to a woman who believes in giving good gifts as tokens of affection.

In marriage, couples engage in this balancing dance of opposites. Where at the start, both happen to be spenders, one eventually assumes the role of super-spender, the other the role of a super-saver. A spender when not spending feels deprived. A saver when not spending feels virtuous. Evidently, few marriages can survive two super-spenders. Eventually couples start operating a system of checks and balances. Similarly, if both happen to be hoarders, one often blossoms into a mild spender while the other hardens in the worrier role. Their living could turn nasty if both stayed super-misers.

Ironically, the longer couples are married, the more they lock into polarized roles. And this confrontation game goes on; each side sticking to its own beliefs on money matters.

These days, we have cases where a wife may be earning more than her hubby does. This can pose problems for the male ego; successful wives, threatened husbands. To many a husband the situation is acceptable because it raises the couple's standard of living. Men quite often are choosing partners on their earning potential, rather than their looks.

Between old couples, many an elderly wife is prone to be a saver than a spender. Usually, her husband is a few years older. And if he happens to be suffering from a serious health problem, such as heart disease, acute diabetes, or any other ailment which endangers his life, the wife thereby is worried about years of widowhood. In such a situation, she seeks the strength of money (including a residential home in her name) for an independent existence. The anticipated support from the progeny could well be tiresome, even humiliating, if at all forthcoming. For the older women, money possibly becomes her best option to live a life of acceptable independence. Mostly, her first priority is to have an undisputed title of a home where she can live, even earn some income from renting a part of it.

Much advice is coming forth these days on the subject of money in marriage. Yet you have to work out your own particular money relationship. You are two unique individuals and you fit together in your own unique way. And conflicts about money can only begin to be resolved if you start realising that the other person is an entirely separate person from you in every way, no matter how romantic your love is, or how long you have been married.

Experts, however, do agree over a few points.

- Crucially, couples need to learn to listen to each other, to minimize fights about money. Corinne Sweet in her book *Stop Fighting About Money* (Hodder and Houthen, 2000) favours a periodic listening exercise: Agree to listen to each other on money matters for five minutes—by the watch—without interruption. Sit comfortably facing each other in a room you won't be interrupted by phone or people coming in. One partner talks for full five minutes, the other listens—keep eye contact but do not interrupt, comment, laugh, nod, agree, or prompt. When the time is up, swap over.

- Don't talk about money when you are angry. The irony is that most couples only deal with the issue of money when they are fighting.
- Concentrate money talk on the future, or talk about what's going on. It is no use raking the past; you would never agree about the past.
- Debt is the marriage monster. When couples get into debt, it creates stress, worry, frustration, and fear. And the worst relationship scenario when you can't pay back a loan from your in-laws. The couple needs to take charge of the situation—otherwise love dies. And do not borrow from each other, unless it's absolutely clear about the terms of borrowing. Then you must pay back the borrowed money in stipulated or agreed time. Any failings here can mean a lot of ammunition building up for money fights.

The Money Equation

In forty years of marriage, Ravinder and Reema have seen a sea change in their money equation. For the first twenty years, Ravi was the sole breadwinner. In the next fifteen, Ravi continued as a principal earner but Reema, running a beauty parlour, began contributing an increasing share. For the last 5 years, Ravi is retired and has no income except his pension and rent from a flat, while Reema's beauty parlour is doing a booming business.

Now Ravi only buys his own clothes, pays for petrol, and settles outside payments like club bills and insurance premiums. Everything else, all expenses on food, servants' salaries, and sundry purchases—and these constitute their major spending—are met by Reema.

Initially, they had gone along with the traditional approach of "our money". Gradually, the concept of "my money" as different from "your money" has crept in. Reema now keeps separate accounts.

Yet somewhere deep in the irrational layers of her psyche, she still thinks of the man as the prime breadwinner, the obvious one to pick up the tab. Indeed at times, she guiltily slips money to Ravi under the restaurant table so that he can pretend he is paying.

The disparity in their styles of life manifests itself in trivial ways. For example, although Ravi is quite happy with an old suit, she is forcing a replacement by gifting him an expensive one on his birthday. She wanted to go to Oberoi (Italian restaurant) on their marriage anniversary dinner, he advocating a cheaper meal at their club. Reema often tries to play down such differences, but to her, money has become a luminous symbol of functionality and power. All this leaves Ravi a bit confused and unsure of himself—not a promising scenario for marital harmony.

Between marriage partners, money is always a partner, too. And money issues are relatively harder to resolve, as couples often fail to explore their money beliefs.

Among couples where both are independent earners, there often creeps up another curious phenomenon; that of staying rather secretive about their earnings. Take Mohan and Malti, he, a doctor having a flourishing private practice, she a successful income tax law practitioner. They are a loving open-minded, imaginative couple. They have been together for nearly twenty years. They are not actually revealing to each other about their earnings and bank balances. This might seem unusual, yet something similar may well be obtaining in many marriages. That way money is the last taboo. Among friends again, we may be happy to confide our innermost secrets, but when it comes to revealing how much we earn or save, most of us are less forthcoming.

Men and women, even otherwise, harbour different approaches to money, and these can complicate marital relations. For example, in evolutionary terms, men evolved as hunters, women as gatherers. Men often display the hunter's approach: they go out, buy a pair of shoes, and wear them out. When they die, the man goes out and gets another pair. Women, in contrast, gather. Many times, they buy things not for immediate use but to store these for future occasions.

Despite advances in gender equality and the rising number of women with independent incomes, men are still bred to believe they are better at dealing with money. Women are mostly raised to believe they won't be good at it, but with luck, they may get some man who will take care of the details of money and investments.

Another important difference between men and women concerns their approach to merging their money. Typically, men want to merge all the couple's money, on which they hope to retain primary decision-making power. Women want at least some money separate. This they want as an expression of their healthy autonomy.

A common strategy employed by two-income couples is to merge a portion of their income for joint expenses—the ratio of contribution whether 50:50 or anything else, depending entirely on what they earn. The balance of income is kept separate where your partner doesn't have much say about how you spend it. This can avert quite a few money conflicts.

Marriage experts advise that couples hold frequent 'money meetings', at least once every fortnight. Such negotiations, it is said, can prove a catalyst for learning and growth—even intimacy. Money has a way of bringing any relationship down to a very concrete level.

And it must be understood that the partner with most money typically ends up having the most say.

Money and Happiness

Money, money, money. Everyone wants it, wants more than what he/she has, wants more than others. To millions, money is everything. Indeed, we could be getting into the grip of a money mania.

Surely, money, and the good things money can buy, is a necessary condition of happiness. At the minimum, money wards off the misery and unhappiness that comes with want.

How much money is enough for happiness? Different people will come up with widely varying answers. To some, there is no such thing as having too much of money, with all the depredations of inflation and taxes. Others are inclined to believe that money beyond a certain point can actually complicate life rather than improve it. Several studies have revealed that big winners of lotteries were not appreciably happier after a year or two of their win.

Acquisition of more and more money has this implication; your adaptation level goes up. The kind of lifestyle you expect drifts upward. Things like big houses, expensive cars, luxury travel become routine. Almost inexorable laws of diminishing returns come into operation. Enjoyable activities tend to lose their savour with repetition, thus making their beneficial effect short-lived.

The world, for example, is teeming with people who feel compelled to count pennies when there's no practical need for them to scrimp, or who often find that bitter disagreements about money strain their friendships, their bonds with family members, even their marriage.

Apparently money can't buy happiness. Then what else can guarantee it? Seemingly, there is no single, simple mantra for happiness.

A host of factors are said to contribute to happiness. Health, youth, a happy marriage, a cheerful disposition, meaningful work, and an active social life are some of the ingredients—necessarily backed by a reasonable amount of money.

Physical fitness is evidently conducive to happiness, yet physically handicapped persons are not precluded from happiness, once they have got over the trauma of their handicap.

Common sense suggests that younger people should be happier than older ones. Yet the link between age and happiness has been found to be relatively weak. Older people usually have a smaller discrepancy between aspiration and achievement, because their experiences of life have taught them to be realistic about what can be achieved. One recent study revealed that many people selected a time within five years of their present age as the happiest for them.

Surveys show that marriage seems to prevent people from becoming unhappy. Marriage does so mainly by sharing problems and preventing loneliness. Yet it would make little sense to argue that marriage itself proves a panacea for happiness. Money issues pose particular problems in marital relationships. They're hard to talk about and harder to resolve. Possibly the best way to tackle them is to put yourself in your partner's place.

Happiness, it is said, is more a question of *disposition* than *position*, something even genetic. We may feel euphoric over some good news or be miserable over a bad one, but we soon revert to our usual self; the discontented go back to becoming morose, the sunny-natured continue cheerful. The change in circumstances merely causes a blip in the predictable graph of our lives.

Can you do anything to actively promote happiness? Experts are agreed that the best recipe is to keep oneself busy; busy people are almost always happy. Anyway, caught up in their activities, they are too busy to be unhappy. They have less time for introspection, and it's introspection that often chases away happiness.

It is again a good idea to get interested in other people instead of focusing all the time on one's own problems. People whose main concern is their own happiness seldom find it.

"No man is happy who does not feel happy," said the Roman emperor Marcus Aurelius. Some present-day experts go further; they advise you to feign happiness if you don't feel like it. Fake optimism. Simulate outgoingness. The whole thing may sound phony but before long the pretence would diminish, our changed behaviour could ignite a spark—the spark leading to happiness.

Earn-and-Spend Syndrome

The earn-and-spend syndrome—a mutually reinforcing and powerful syndrome—is a middle-class affliction of modern times. And the ranks of the middle class have been swelling everywhere in recent times.

What exactly is middle class? Economists continue to differ. And what is middle class in developed countries could well define our Indian upper class. In the current context, our middle class could possibly include families with annual incomes ranging from Rs. 8 lakh to Rs. 24 lakh. The way things are shaping up with inflation, the sums could go considerably higher.

We are fast becoming a consumer-oriented society. There is the restless yearning to own more and more goods that impart style and status besides adding to one's enjoyment of life. That necessarily implies making more money, by hard work or otherwise. No wonder it has given rise to such widespread corruption, dowry demands, and a host of other sharp practices.

Consumerism is not an historical trait of human nature, but a product of capitalism. As the market system gains in vigour, consumerism spills over beyond the rich. The growth of the middle classes creates large numbers of potential buyers who see the prospects of elevated status through copying patterns of ownership and consumption set up by the rich.

Consumerism has perhaps reached its apogee in the United States, the country with the most capitalistic and consumer-oriented society in history.

No doubt, consumerism triggers greater economic activity and a higher efficiency thereof. Yet rampant consumerism exacts its own price; the avid consumer has to work much harder to pay for it. That explains why Americans work significantly longer hours as compared to, say, the French or the Italians. Millions are working overtime or on second jobs. Two-thirds of American women of working age are at work, mainly to meet heightened demands. Demands not of essentials like food—food is cheap and abundant in that country—but of things that make us feel superior to our fellows: better and bigger houses, more and classier cars, high-tech refrigerators, washing machines, kitchen ranges, air-conditioners, dishwashers, microwaves, TVs, music systems, and a multiplicity of other appliances and gadgets. And buying many more services, such as foreign travel, restaurant meals, hair and skin care, and umpteen products of the leisure and sports industries.

The insidious cycle of earn-and-spend goes on relentlessly, the family wants always staying ahead of its resources. The syndrome often leads to stress, anxiety, even depression.

Rising incomes, coupled with rising expectations, are obviously the essential facets of consumerism. Yet what has largely triggered modern consumerism is the pressure salesmanship of the capitalist manufacturing and distributive industry. This pressure is mostly exerted through advertisements.

The role of advertising is not just that of "the hidden persuader" or simply informing people about the competing merits of diverse products and brands. It serves the 'culture of wanting', and legitimizes all wants; making whim, caprice and need indistinguishable. Lives of human beings are supposed to take on a borrowed luster from what they buy, in the same way that the moon borrows the light of sun.

The advertising industry employs some of the most powerful and effective words and images to push its message. The three magic words now in constant use are *new, improved* and *free.* All the time they are flashed before the consumer until they settle somewhere in his mind.

Television, the most powerful deliverer of advertising messages, specializes in showing how lives can be exalted or made complete by the acquisition of promoted goods or services. Television's animation particularly lures children. The advertisers are now only pressure-selling things that children directly use like sweets, soft drinks and toys, but through children, especially through teenagers, pressurize parents to buy particular brands of two-wheelers, computers, and various household gadgets.

Ads are everywhere you go or see—on billboards, lampposts, covers of scooter stepneys, backs of bus tickets, and shirts of professional cricket players. Ads at all imaginable places and on an infinite variety of products.

We are, it seems, in for a rapid and sustained rise in consumerism. It is in the very nature of capitalism to produce more and more consumer goods, and find buyers for these. And it excites consumer demand through an avalanche of ads. One of its standard approaches is to make the consumer somewhat dissatisfied with the goods he is using so that he buys "improved" ones.

5

Children in Marriage

Childless by Choice

These days you occasionally hear the phrase "child-free" instead of "childless". To some it almost smacks of eradication like "smoke free" or "pest free". Those who use it make out that "childless" has connotations of loss or regret; "child-free" implies satisfaction and deliberate choice. To be child-free, they argue, means giving far more thought to not having children than most parents give to having children.

Until recent times, childlessness was simply assumed to be an involuntary condition, caused by infertility—the same now increasingly amenable to scientific advances in the fertility field. Voluntary childlessness goes so much against the grain of normative behaviour; the traditional transitions of a woman's life as she shifts from single woman to wife to mother to grandmother.

For centuries, women didn't really have a choice—if they were sexually active, and most of them were—then they would become mothers. Yet there has always been a tiny segment of the population whose absence of offspring was intentional.

Moreover, this childlessness by choice is clearly on the rise in upwardly mobile societies and groups, more so with career-oriented women. "Parenthood is on the backburner, career in the microwave," said the sexologist Prakash Kothari. Urban working couples are hitting the pause button when it comes to conception, either from the disruption a child would cause to their career or not enough money to raise children the way they want. This pause sometimes becomes so long, complications may arise when they want to conceive.

To many child-free votaries, it's an honourable choice. They seem to do no real heart-searching about not having children, no regrets.

Jean E.Veevers' book *Childless by Choice* (Butterworth), discusses the making of a non-parent. In many cases, childlessness is seen more as an evolving state than a sudden decision. Only one-third of her sample had made the decision before marriage. The other two-thirds arrived at their choice by a series of stages, beginning with several successive postponements of intended parenthood.

Yet they were using contraceptives effectively from the start. After successive postponements came a period of explicit consideration of pros and cons. In half the cases one partner convinced the reluctant other, and in the remainder the decision was mutual.

Asked about reasons for their decision, freedom was uniformly cited as the overriding advantage; more freedom in the use of time and the use of money.

The popular perception that childless women had a morbid fear of childbirth was not generally borne out. Do childless women dislike children? Some of those interviewed felt that they would not be good mothers because of failings of patience or their temper. But overall, only half reported they actually did not like children. Some indeed had special relationships with little nieces or nephews. Others in their professional capacity as teachers or nurses did extensive work with children.

Laurie Lisle in her book *Without Child* (Ballantine Books) concedes that child tending builds self-confidence and develops capacity for patience and responsibility. However, she finds that middle-aged women, mothers or not, base their feelings of wellbeing on success in their work and pleasure in marriage; other aspects such as the presence of children are less crucial. Again she finds that elderly non-mothers tended to be more resourceful, self-reliant and gifted at friendship than their counterparts.

Child-free couples (excluding the biologically barren) tend to evoke disapproval if not hostility, from relatives and friends, even from strangers. They are deemed selfish or emotionally immature. Some critics even question whether adults who intended no children should marry at all.

The whole debate can be distilled down to the word "selfish". The childless by choice are deemed selfish. Though "selfishness" is rarely spelled out, it may imply things such as the childless spending money on vain pleasures, even enhanced sexual activity the child-free are presumed to enjoy. The childless are told that if no one had children, there would be no more society. Paradoxically, those who make this accusation simultaneously believe that the childless miss out on the deepest, if not the greatest, joy known to human beings.

Non-parents counter the "selfish" charge saying that overpopulation is a bigger problem than under-population, and that parents rarely decide to be parents out of a perceived obligation to humankind. Parents have children, non-parents say, because they are selfish—because they want a baby to coo over or a genetic link to the future, or a prop for their old age.

Wives invite greater pressure as well as censure for the child-free condition; they are assumed either career-crazed or spinster types if not deviant. Only greatly creative women aren't expected to have children—writers, poets, painters—if their abilities were revealed early enough.

As having or not having children affects the lives of wives more, childlessness is viewed as essentially dependent upon the woman's decision and determination. Little wonder, there is the general tendency to neglect the study of childless husbands.

How do the child-free handle the situation when quizzed about their intentional childlessness? Most of the respondents report considerable practice in suiting their reasons to the audience; giving one justification out of a complex of reasons to parents or grandparents, another to colleagues or friends, another to strangers. Some couples deflect criticism by announcing an intention to adopt.

And the child-free respond to criticism in various ways, ranging from cheerful acceptance to guilty defensiveness, from thoughtful discussion to a brusque reply. The women's responses are usually more diffident. Some readily admit to "indulging themselves disgracefully". Others may well retort, "What's wrong in being selfish?" Money is seldom given as a reason for refusing the responsibilities of parenthood.

What about child-free couples in their old age? Won't they be impoverished without the support and companionship of children? And who will carry the family name after their demise?

In this context, it has to be noted that couples childless by choice are on the average better educated and more career-oriented. And are usually well-off to be financially independent in their old age. Even otherwise, some studies have shown that these days older people in their 60s and 70s are more likely to help their children financially than the other way around.

Again, many of the elderly these days are preferring to live on their own than move in with their children. They may well engage professionals to provide healthcare than be a burden to their busy children. However, the non-parent's sense of loneliness could become acute when one of the partner dies. The childless elderly try to make up with more active social life and hobbies. A few studies have thrown up an astonishing finding: elder non-parents tend to be happier and healthier than their counterparts.

The Only Child

"I can spot an only child at twenty paces. It is something about the space they always need," says David Emerson, the co-author of *Only Child* (Souvenir Press). He and Jill Pitkeathley had interviewed in depth hundreds of adults who were onlies.

"Having all those goodies, all that undiluted parental attention, not having to share with other siblings, missing out on rough and tumble of a sibling childhood—and many more distinct experiences—does create in the only child someone special, someone with behaviour that can seem strange to those who have grown up amongst brothers and sisters", say the authors.

Being surrounded by adult company and being the centre of attraction, the child quickly develops a larger vocabulary and models his behaviour on adults around him. Parents increasingly give him responsible tasks and involve him in decision-making about the house and family. Indeed, being the focus of attention can be a very good childhood experience, generating self-confidence.

The undivided attention of both parents means that whatever you say is likely to be heard. The moment his foot crosses the door there's a parent saying, "Hello, how are you? Has it been a good day?" The situation is clearly different where three or more siblings are clamouring for parental attention.

'Only' children get more parental support in education than what is available to children with siblings. Parents indulge them more in their hobbies; concerned that the only child wouldn't get bored.

Yet there are negative aspects, too. When onlies play with other children, their lack of experience in joining in can hold them back and make them appear standoffish. Onlies just haven't been used to the jostling and bumping up against each other that is common among other children. And onlies find it difficult to cope with teasing that goes on in schools—they have no such experience at home.

They are often unable to deal with anger in a light-hearted or non-threatening manner because they never had the squabbling, bickering and then forgetting it as most children have.

Relating to brother and sister and having to accommodate them, howsoever reluctantly, is an invaluable training for later life. Surely you can get by without it; you can even learn some of it. But what siblings do provide is an emotional training for life that is difficult, if not impossible, to replicate.

No brothers and sisters to borrow or move things. 'Only' children can retain a burning resentment at other people's thoughtless rearrangement of their territory. Borrowing without asking and putting them in the wrong places make the 'only' children (even when grown up) really angry.

The greater time and attention available from a parent means that the only child's needs tend to met fully and quickly. As a consequence, onlies often develop a sense of immediacy. They want things to happen quickly and are usually more restive in queues.

Being in the limelight for a few years is something first-born children may share with onlies, and may explain some of their shared characteristics. But for the only child, of course, this focus is never shattered.

Any talk of onlies brings in China. The country's one-child policy is the most ambitious piece of social engineering in history. Never has any nation attempted something as drastic and of such magnitude as this policy. What will be all its ramifications for the Chinese society? And what about the coming crop of only children; only children born to parents who themselves were single children?

With son-preference strong in the Han Chinese (akin to ours), the one-child regime operated harshly on girls. Yet, unintended as it may be, the one-child policy has done wonders to the status and image of Chinese girls. Millions of middle-class urban families now have one girl child. Parents dote on them, prize them. These girls are receiving almost as much parental attention and investment in their education as single sons. The one-child policy seems to have triggered a silent revolution, leading to greater girl-acceptance and a boost to women's self-esteem in a traditionally male-oriented society.

In the early 1980s, various Chinese research psychologists found that the only children—"the little emperors"—were more likely to have personality and social behavioural problems. They grow more stubborn, moody, irritable, less sharing than non-only children.

Another consequence: these onlies are usually overfed, many to the point of obesity. Whatever they want—and they mostly demand foods rich in fats and proteins, such as meats, sweets and fast-foods—they are given. Grandparents are even more indulgent; they tend to cater to every whim of the grandchild. No wonder, single children are known in Chinese as "four-two-one": four grandparents, two parents, and one spoiled brat.

Besides spending relatively large sums on over-feeding their onlies, parents are seen to spare no expense on their toys and clothes. In many families nearly half the family budget is snapped up by the only.

The parents often go to extraordinary lengths to give the only child the best possible education. That's the top priority, no matter what it costs. Special tutors are hired for studies after schools. Parents skimp on their own consumption, take loans, to buy the only child expensive educational inputs, such as a computer, even a piano.

No wonder quite a few Chinese surveys concluded that only children were more egocentric, with lower ratings in cooperation than non-only children. Elsewhere in the world the only-child situation doesn't go beyond the concerns of individual family happiness and the child's psychological adjustment.

Some prejudice against the only child is age-old in every culture. Popular sentiment still persists that a second child is needed to provide companionship to the first, so that the first won't be spoiled or be selfish or feel lonesome. Parents experience pressure from relatives and friends to have a second child—sometimes even more pressure than to have the first.

The only child, however, is faring well in western research. These studies concentrate on IQ and school results, items lending themselves to more accurate quantification than the vague 'personality'. When it comes to educational achievements, the results are clear-cut; only children have been found to have higher achievements in both length of education and quality of academic work.

As to personality traits such as emotional adjustment and sociability, western research generally finds no significant difference between only and non-only children—the only children "more maligned than maladjusted". It is not the nature of only children that creates problems, but what is expected of them by their families and society. If they are any different, it is because of the heightened expectations and anxieties that others have about them.

In India, there has been a steady rise in single-child couples. A growing number of our matrimonial ads highlight that the boy or girl in question has the advantage of being an only child.

In recent years a new perspective on only children is emerging. The most noted researcher in this field is Tony Falbo, a professor of educational psychology at the University of Texas. She (herself an only) has conducted numerous surveys and examined more than a hundred studies done since the 1920s.

Falbo concludes that only children scored significantly better than other groups in achievement, motivation and personal adjustment, and were in all other respects indistinguishable from children with siblings.

The debate, however, still goes on about the advantages and disadvantages of being the only child.

Latecomers: Children Born to Older Parents

Satish, a 40-year-old business executive, was born when his father was forty-eight and his mother thirty-nine. At his birth, two sisters were fifteen and thirteen. Satish says his parents just wouldn't give up the idea of having a son.

"By the time I was twelve, my father had grown bald and my mother was grayish. I felt a little embarrassed when I saw my parents next to other kids' at school functions. They always seemed less active; I don't remember my father playing any ball games with me.

I was uncle to half a dozen nephews by the time I was in first grade. There were no grandparents to go to, and my sisters were motherly.

By the time I was thirty-five, I was deep into caring for my sick mother, my father dying already after a protracted illness."

Renu, a young physician, was born when her father was thirty-nine and her mother thirty-eight. She is the only child of parents who are both doctors.

"By the time I arrived in this world, my parents were successful professionals and moneyed. I had a marvelous childhood. They took me on many trips and gave me lots of toys and books. Moreover, my mother, I believe, taught me early to be self-reliant and career-oriented, with her talk and example. I rate myself lucky for being born to parents who were already mature."

Social scientists have rarely given thought to the influences that shape latecomers—children born to mothers over 35 and fathers often much older, whereas children of divorced parents, working mothers, alcoholic parents, adoptive parents have been extensively investigated.

The effects of birth order have again been researched, with firstborns and onlies receiving special attention.

Evidently having older parents does make a difference. But this difference has yet to be studied in scientific terms. Is it a hazard or an advantage? Is the latecomers' childhood different from those of children born to parents in their twenties? And does this feeling of being different continue from childhood into adulthood?

Andrew L. Yarrow, a *New York Times* reporter had attempted to answer some of these questions. He queried hundreds of Americans who had been born to older parents. He summed up their reactions, along with his comments, in the book *Latecomers: Children of Parents Over 35* (Free Press). The book makes interesting reading.

Children are born to older parents either by chance or by choice. There are those who are the result of an 'accident' or 'mistake'; the last in the line of children, born with a gap of years separating them from their next older sibling. And when they learn they had been unwanted, this knowledge usually hurts. While some receive lots of attention as the 'baby' of the family, others prove weary to their older parents who had planned on settling down to a well-defined life after the close of the child-rearing phase. This sort of perceived parental resentment of their children's intrusion into their lives could continue, in some cases, long after childhood. Anyway, these cases are set to decline with the prevalence of more reliable contraceptives.

Another category is the long-awaited ones, with couples trying for years to get a child. When such babies arrive, they are the subject of much parental doting. Whether the same does them any great good is another matter.

Then are those children whose coming had been delayed because of conscious family planning or of a late marriage itself. The latter can be a significant feature in marriages of the divorced or widowed. Again, we have instances of famous men over sixty marrying much younger women and producing children: celebrities such as Pablo Picasso, Jomo Kenyatta, and writers Kurt Vonnegut and Leon Uris come to mind.

Of course, a good deal will depend on a latecomer's particular circumstances and the family situation. Yet latecomers seem to encounter some typical problems and privileges.

The generation gap between the older parents and their offspring is wider. Children often feel that their parents are too conservative, outdated and set in their ways. The generation gap typically worsens during adolescence. Teenagers may feel that the ideas of their older parents on clothes, entertainment and dating are too out-dated or rigid.

On the other hand, older parents being more mature and experienced, can be calmer, more tolerant, more understanding. Again, older parents are more likely to be economically secure and emotionally stable.

This can yield high-quality parenting.

There's an old saying: "Old people have old babies". Many children of older parents tend to feel, they "grew up fast".

They imagine they were treated more like adults and given more responsibility than their friends with younger parents.

The older parents are apt to communicate with their children in ways that are more "adult". Again, older parents, it seems, are involved in mature pastimes like reading and music, instead of games and other robust physical activities. Their interests frequently are passed on to their children.

As older parents are often too intense at child rearing, the children are under greater pressure to perform than those born to younger parents. These kids are likely to have fewer siblings. They will be more individualistic, type-A achievers.

For many latecomers, right in the busy prime of their lives they are called upon to take care of their ageing parents. And this care-giving can be especially difficult when there are no brothers or sisters to share the burden. Often there are no grandparents in the lives of latecomers, and this can evoke some regret.

Till recently, the normative ideal was that it is best to become a parent in one's twenties. Indeed, older parents begetting children were the subject of snide remarks. Medically again, mothers were advised that childbirth in late thirties carried more risks to the mother and child.

Social attitudes seem to be changing. People are marrying late; others are delaying children for career considerations or other personal reasons. It is also made out in defence that people today are "young" longer; the dividing line between youth and middle age pushed back from thirty to forty.

Women in their late thirties and forties are still considered high-risk mothers by some obstetricians, but new medical knowledge and procedures has led to changes in perspectives on these "elderly" thirty-five plus. Advances in obstetrics certainly play a role in reducing the perception that later childbearing is 'wrong'. Actually, many older parents get the feel of being young again when a child is born to them.

In some professional circles, late childbirth is being deemed as something more chic than deviant. And this trend could well accelerate in coming years. Increasingly, career women are delaying children till they have established themselves in their calling. However, this could also trigger a certain anxiety, even panic, when they reach the now-or-never stage, the biological clock ticking remorselessly against them.

While older parents commonly derive much satisfaction and pleasure from latecomers, whether latecomers themselves are better off having older parents is not that clear. The emerging picture is rather mixed, with some children coming out as gainers and others as losers. And there are those for whom the gains and losses balance out.

How Significant is Your Birth Order?

The birth-order gurus claim they can predict your personality from your birth order.

The birth-order theory is built around the appealingly simple idea that your place in the family determines your strengths and failings, your mental make-up.

According to it, if you were the first-born or the only born, you received the full charge of your parents' attention and expectations. That made you demanding, self-centred, somewhat over controlling, and ambitious. The oldest or the single child tends to spend more time with adults. This is one reason why such children are likely to develop faster, and show greater eagerness to assume leadership or responsible roles.

Jawaharlal Nehru, that way, had to be the first-born. And Indira Gandhi, the only born. The intensive early education of John Stuart Mill at the behest of his great father was largely a product of the same situation.

The personalities of middle children are harder to define or classify. However, they do suffer some benign neglect; they have fewer pictures in the family album. To cope with the lack of parental attention, they tend to become rebellious and secretive. As they never get their parents all to themselves, they learn to compromise, act more accommodating.

At its best, the process can make them more sensitive, more human. The poets, Tennyson and Tagore, were middle children.

What about the last-born? By the time they are born—frequently born unplanned—their parents have mostly exhausted their expectations of children; this could make the last-born smoulder with thwarted ambition. Parents are content to pamper the youngest one almost unreservedly. Last-born are described variously as clowns and cutups. They often act more spoiled than the onlies.

Some birth-order experts, to prove their point, make out that many of the world's comedians and clowns were the last-born.

Leman, the author of *The Birth Order Book*, is the reigning guru. His main argument is that the dynamics between the parents and the children plays a crucial part in the formation of personality, and here the order of one's birth matters a lot. "You can use birth-order to get a quick handle on people," says he. Freud is quoted as saying that "a child's position in the sequence of brothers and sisters is of very great significance for the course of his later life".

The Austrian family therapist, Walter Toman, author of *Family Constellation: Its Effects on Personality and Social Behaviour*, has done the most authoritative work on birth order. Toman's basic assertion is that the order of one's birth determines certain personality characteristics that shape the choices we make and the likelihood of our success and even how we think about ourselves.

All in all, the birth-order theory is now drawing more flak than appreciation, particularly from the scientific community. It is likened more to palm reading or astrology. Even Alfred Adler, the founding father of birth-order theory, believed that it could be carried too far.

"Most serious researchers have stopped talking about birth order," says Falbo. A family is a densely woven fabric made up of innumerable threads; the birth order is just a thread in that carpet.

Suppose there is a wide gap between the second and the third child. Wouldn't be the third child likely to develop the characteristics of a first-born? What· about the second child sharing the traits of the last-born? What happens if the first-born was a boy and the rest all girls? Wouldn't the oldest girl develop a first-born personality in relation to her sisters? And what about the eldest son whose older brother died young? The variations are far too many to draw any hard and fast rules. The family life and child development is too complex a field to lend itself to standard formulae.

Yet the popular appeal of birth-order theory persists. People continue to feel there is something in it.

A First-Time Father

Five years after marriage, the dual-career couple decided to go in for a child. Here are some musings of a first-time father:

One evening we made a ceremony out of retiring all birth control paraphernalia, and jumped into bed. Now that the sex was real, and not just for entertainment, it seemed a scarier proposition. "Look, we'll just be casual about it," I said. "Good idea, we'll see what happens," says Renu. However, there was something eerie in our not trying not to get pregnant. Fortunately, for the human race, God has shrewdly linked procreation to an act that makes men stupid with excitement.

Then one day, Renu reported a suspected pregnancy—she had missed two periods. Soon tests confirmed the pregnancy.

I began feeling a certain sense of power, being a potential father—I was a "fertile man". Now I would make my way across the neighbourhood with a perceptible strut. After all, I had been successful in fulfilling the most basic function of my gender.

As the pregnancy advanced, I became more and more protective of my wife and the foetus she was carrying. Going out with her to the market and other crowded places, I was like a black cat, eyes darting everywhere, scanning the surroundings for anything that smacked of trouble; a hurrying shopper whose bulky bag could swipe her swollen belly or a broken sidewalk that could throw her off balance. People seemed considerate seeing a bulging belly. Even restaurants were quick to give us seats. I suppose one is eyed a little enviously: that person did that to the woman, a pronouncement to the world that the two clearly had sex.

We decided early on to let the sex of the child be a surprise. After all, we had all our lives to know the sex. And once we know it, no way we were going to forget it. So why not keep the suspense for a while. We drew up two parallel lists of names of boys and girls. And collected baby items that could be used by either sex. Even the child's room was decorated keeping the duality in mind.

We bought all sorts of books on pregnancy, birth and child rearing. And some books we got as gifts. Friends whose kids were older now dropped off a few. Aboard the Pregnancy Train, my education accelerated. Once I knew next to nothing about it. Now words like "placenta", "uterus", "ovaries" and "vaginal" were popping in and out of my conversation.

Then the day arrived at the hospital. As is proper for modern would-be fathers, I was asked to be there in the delivery room. But when Renu started writhing in birth pangs, I could take it no more. I can't even watch a child being vaccinated. I slipped out, leaving her mother there with the doctors. Waiting for the childbirth, I went through every emotion there is: joy, fear, love, anger, and helplessness, wonder . . . .

Out came the doctor gleefully pronouncing, "It's a boy". A boy! Yes! I was thrilled. To be frank, I wished for a boy. Now I was prepared to confess the same to myself and to others. Throughout pregnancy, we had simply kept on saying, "We just want a healthy child". But when it happened to work out my way, there was no way to pretend I was not smiling a teeny bit wider.

A new child in the house is a huge tourist attraction. Everybody has to come, everybody has to see it, hold it, and to comment which parent the child resembles. I was behaving overtly protective, "Okay, you have to wash your hands before you can handle the baby. . . . You have to remove any sharp objects to be found on your person or clothing". Asking people to keep quiet when he was asleep, as if I had become the world's librarian.

For the next few months, the most striking element of parenthood was sleep deprivation. Indeed, when you are the parent of a new child, all the craving and desire you have ever felt for sex is transferred over to sleep. "It's like somebody sneaked into your brain, found the wires to the sex button and the sleep button, and just switched them," says one first-time father.

And with sleep deprivation, certain crankiness crept in. Just when we needed each other most, we often found ourselves snapping at each other.

Several months pass. The baby now sleeps in an adjoining room. And mercifully, he has started sleeping the whole night through. Time for the first-time parents to switch back to their routine of sleep and lovemaking.

Choosing the Sex of Children

Almost no subject is more steeped in myth and lore than the business of choosing the sex of children. Aristotle recommended placing the bed on a north–south axis for those wanting boys. Various diets or drugs have been advocated through centuries for producing male children.

Yet the only sure way to be certain of having a boy has been, sadly, female infanticide; newborn girls killed through poisoning, throttling, plain starvation or neglect. This gruesome practice should be on decline as science has come up with new ways of knowing the sex of the unborn child, coupled with easier and safer forms of abortion. Various studies have shown that in our country, around 99% of the induced abortions were of females.

The induction of ultrasound equipment meant to detect serious and fatal diseases is now being widely misused to get rid of female foetuses. Female infanticide through use of ultrasound machine has taken the shape of a serious menace in the country despite the efforts by the authorities to check the same. Ultrasound can image foetal genitals as early as 14 weeks.

If human beings do acquire the capacity to choose the sex of their offspring, a host of ethical questions will arise. And these will have no easy answers till women attain equal status with men. There is nothing inherently wrong in human beings acquiring an ability to choose the sex of their children—in fact, the choice will be another gift of science to enrich human life. Then, the widespread operation of such a choice calls for acclimate of essential equality between the two sexes.

Suffering is Mostly for Women

On an average, husbands in India going for vasectomy do not form even 1% of the wives going for tubectomy. The tubectomy is a far more complicated than the vasectomy. The latter is a simple procedure and is even reversible.

Obviously, our couples when they decide to control births through surgical intervention are mostly opting out for the more complicated operation for the wife than the simpler one for the husband. What could be the rationale behind such a seemingly weird choice?

It is usually explained on the male apprehensions of an impotency or some loss of virility. Others are said to be held back for the fear, if their wife died or got divorced—the latter event less likely in our Indian conditions, they won't be in a position to produce an issue with the next wife. Or is it simply a case of escaping contact with a surgeon's knife when the object can be achieved by shifting the onus on to one's wife? After all she is well acclimatized to pain, discomfort and bleeding through years of menstruation (the human female is the only mammal that menstruates monthly, she ovulates throughout the year and not at particular seasons like other animals), burdensome periods of pregnancy and the childbirths—perhaps also a couple of abortions or a cesarean. In the context of putting up with physical pain, women seem to be the stronger sex.

Are these factors enough to produce the alarming imbalance between the number of tubal ligations and vasectomies performed in the country? Or is it all due to the greater motivation of women to avoid unwanted births? "Men never think, at least seldom think, what a hard task it is for us women to go through childbirths very often," rued Queen Victoria.

Some way it is to be blamed on the basic selfishness of men (this expression is being used for want of a better one) or their enhanced importance of what happens to them. Men would like to do without "the spoilsport" condoms in marital sex, though the condoms have vastly improved; these are thinner, lubricated, even perfumed and coloured. So it often means the wife taking to birth-control pills with all the attendant risks that go with interference with the natural body processes. Or have an intrauterine device (IUD) fitted in, and become "the grumbling loop wife" with chances of pelvic inflammation. And finally she gets pushed into the more difficult and dangerous operation of tubectomy instead of his undergoing vasectomy. And mind you, all this in a field of activity which is patently more pleasurable to men—generally more sought after by men—than to their spouses.

In men's defence perhaps it can be argued that vasectomy and tubectomy is nearly the same thing. In vasectomy, the vas deferens, the duct passing sperm from the testes to the prostrate and the penis is severed. In tubectomy again, the uterine tubes (commonly called fallopian tubes after the name of Dr. Gabriel Fallopius, the great Italian anatomist, which is also credited with the invention of a linen condom for the prevention of venereal disease) that carry ova from the ovaries to the uterus are blocked.

Yet there the similarity ends. Vasectomy is a quick, simple operation normally carried out under local anesthesia, and in a doctor's clinic. The vas deferens duct is easily accessible in the exposed scrotum (nature hung the testes out to keep the sperm cooler than the body's temperature). Normal work can be resumed soon after the operation. No long-term adverse effects have been demonstrated in men. Vasectomy leaves the bulk of seminal fluid intact unlike castration.

On the other hand, fallopian tubes lie buried deeply in the female pelvis. To perform sterilization a surgeon must either open the abdomen, in a procedure called a laparotomy, and close the tubes under direct vision, or insert an optical instrument (laparoscope) to view the tubes so that a clip, ring or electrocautery can be applied. The operation is best performed under regular surgical conditions, and often requires a day or two of hospitalization for recuperation and observation.

Anyway, the operation demands far more resources in terms of hospital facilities and surgeons' time—things that are always scarce in countries like ours.

One is not sure whether much can be done to change men's perceptions in this field. Yet it may be a good idea to keep on highlighting the difference between the two operations in a popular media like TV. A better appreciation of the same may generate higher sensitivity on the subject. Admittedly, fewer male sterilizations than female sterilizations have been performed worldwide, but the ratio is something like 1 to 2, not 1 to 100 as in India.

IVF (In Vitro Fertilization)

Twins and Triplets

Infertile couples long for children, spend lot of money on IVF (*in vitro fertilization*), and are gladdened when their efforts bear fruit. Then, many a couple in want of one child is saddled with twins or triplets, something the couple simply had not bargained for.

Currently, one in three IVF births produce multiple babies. Cases of women giving birth to triplets are not uncommon. The epidemic of multiple births arising from fertility treatments is escalating.

Women's bodies are not designed to give birth to a litter. And imagine the impact on the foetuses themselves from sharing those tight quarters.

Multiple births are no longer considered exactly a divine gift or even the result of expensive fertility drugs but something more akin to medical malpractice. In most cases, multiple IVF births are avoidable.

Doctors generally implant more than one embryo in the woman, expecting that not all will develop into pregnancy. IVF procedures being costly, the incentive is to ensure a baby in minimum attempts.

One way to minimize multiple births is to limit by law the number of IVF embryos that can be implanted in the woman at one time. Singapore has a law allowing only two embryos to be put in at one time. Netherlands has gone a step forward; now only one embryo is allowed to be implanted. We have yet to legislate on the subject.

Seeking the Best Sperm

Sperm banking is now global, like any other consumer product or service. The Internet has added a new dimension to artificial insemination: the possibility of viewing a photo of the donor and, in some instances, listening to a tape of his voice. The digital dads seem more like part of a dating service than a medical clinic.

Consumers are no longer limited to the small donor pools locally. The Denmark-based Cryo, for example, is aggressively marketing its product over many countries; it has the avowed goal of becoming the McDonald's of sperm banking.

As recently as 15 years back, a one-line description of the donor was the industry standard. Now, a dozen-page medical and family history is typical.

We have a couple of major sperm banks operating in the country. And their production is said to be enough for meeting the current demand. Yet their donor list remains rather limited, composed mostly of medical students. The donor information as supplied to the intending recipients still stays quite patchy. And unless they upgrade themselves fast to meet the increasingly sophisticated demand for donor sperm in the country, sperm banks from outside with their global reach will infiltrate the home market.

It is estimated that over one-third of artificial insemination practitioners were still using fresh rather than frozen sperm—a procedure highly risk-prone in transmission of disease. Presently, quite often an Indian couple, approaching an IVF centre or a gynaecologist for male infertility, brings along a donor, usually a brother of the husband or even his father or father-in-law, with the idea that family genes would be preferable to outside ones.

Indeed, the whole field of artificial insemination in the country calls for a tightening up, both through legislation and self-regulation by the industry, as the demand for donor sperm is set to register a progressive rise.

The Egg Donors

A sperm donor spends a few minutes in a room that looks like a college boy's fantasy. It has soft-and-hard-core magazines and a comfortable couch under subdued lighting. And he gets paid for an activity that's associated with pleasure.

In contrast, an egg donor faces a gruelling medical regime. She gets fertility drugs injected daily for two weeks. The painful shots cause the woman's moods to swing widely.

The monitoring of egg donors involves daily visits to the clinic for blood tests and ultrasound screening. When the ovaries are ripe, as many as several dozen eggs are harvested with a fifteen-inch-long needle inserted through the vagina. A general or local anesthesia has to be used for the procedure.

Because of the risks presented to women who are recruited to be egg donors, some clinics prefer to use their own IVF patients as egg donors. Since these women are already taking fertility drugs, they seem to face fewer additional physical risks by donating. Some clinics even offer their IVF facilities to women at a reduced cost if they are willing to give some of their eggs to other women.

Lately a special technique has made it possible to freeze eggs for long periods. Once the technique gets refined, women could store eggs in their 20s when they are highly fertile, and use the frozen egg for impregnation, if needed, in later years.

Researchers are focusing on the biological fact that all of a woman's eggs are created prenatal. A woman actually has her maximum number of eggs—about seven million—when she is a twenty-week-old foetus in her mother's womb. By puberty, only around three lakh remain.

Sleepy Teenagers at School Time

Most of our high schools open at eight. The same is the pattern in Europe. In the United States, many schools start at seven. In my student days in the 1940s, our high school, like others, opened at 10 and closed at 4.

At what time schools should open has again become a subject of some debate in various countries.

By the early 1990s, researchers began to find, surprisingly yet consistently, that the sleep patterns of adolescents are discernibly different from those of younger children as well as from adults. At the onset of puberty, there is an alteration in the body clock. Their circadian rhythms, determined by the release of the hormone melatonin and other factors, were telling them to stay up later and to get up later. Teenagers often feel alert into the late hours of the night—well after their elders have collapsed into bed.

From age 12 to 18, we see a steady pushing back of time at which young people go to bed, especially socially active urban teenagers with their CD players, computers and video games. And it could be television, hobbies, or "partying". Anything important or interesting is good enough to push back their bedtime. Indeed, teenagers are biologically incapable of going to bed at a 'sensible' hour.

Parents often experience considerable difficulty in waking up a teenager. While the preadolescent children tend to wake up easily and seem eager to start the day, teenagers usually need several reminders and much prodding to get up. Parents even tell you of times when they actually pushed a teenager out of bed, only to find him asleep on the floor. Sleep-deprived teenagers can be as cranky as tired three-year-olds and even less fun to deal with. The countervailing belief (it is the early bird that gets the worm) that this was largely laziness on the kids' part is rather misplaced.

Researchers have also come to the equally unexpected conclusion that teenagers as a group need more sleep than pre-adolescents—that their bodies and minds require additional unconsciousness to grow best. Being a teenager is itself a tiring business. Studies worldwide indicate that the optimal sleep time for most teenagers was around 9 hours.

Stop waking up teenagers at the crack of dawn, and they just might make better grades in school. That is the latest word from sleep scientists and education experts.

It is in this context that William Demant—the world's leading sleep specialist who discovered REM—makes out that "very early high school start times are not only misguided, they're inherently 'abusive' to many high school kids." Education experts believe an early start best for the needs of younger children, while the later start seems best for high schoolers. Younger children tend to be larks, but from the age of 14, they typically begin to become owls.

No wonder, many a teenager with early school timings—further compounded with long bus rides or long travel time—has been observed to reach school with his or her brain, essentially in sleep-mode.

Subjected to prolonged commuting time, high schoolers often have to get up as early as 6 a.m. In one recent American survey, half of early-rising 10th graders were found to be in the "pathological" range of sleepiness at 8 a.m. "The students may be in school, but their brains are at home on their pillows," says Mary Carkskadon, editor of the book *Adolescent Sleep Patterns* (2002). "There are some kids whose teachers have simply never seen them at their best, and that is a terrible shame."

Researchers have also observed that sleep-deprived kids can't learn as well, and display impaired ability to pay attention, to remember and to do calculations fast. This can prove even more damaging in results when you have to answer examination papers early in the morning.

It has also been found that sleep-debt in teenagers can lead to impulsive behaviour and losing control of the moment; that's when really bad things can happen. And loss of sleep increases teenage drivers' already elevated risk of car accidents.

In the light of these findings, efforts at Congressional level have been made in the United States to change the commonly prevalent high school timings of 8, or 8.30 to 9 or 9.30, with closing time to 4.30 or 5. This would not only give the teenagers an extra hour of sorely-needed sleep but will help keep them off the streets from 4 to 5 p.m., the peak hours for juvenile delinquency. According to Professor Martin Ralph at the

University of Toronto, high schools and universities should ideally start not before 11.

The voices of change include many students (though not all), some parents, and medical and sleep experts. Then any such change is opposed by most teachers (worried it would lengthen their workday), transportation officers (it would raise transport cósts), and coaches (fearing shrinkage of extra curricular activities).

As a result, the move has made little headway, except for some selected schools taking it up on an experimental basis. Nobody seriously challenges the strength of arguments advanced by sleep researchers, whereby teenagers would gain an added hour of sleep as well as get to school when they are 'most ready to learn'. Yet, vested interests and practical difficulties in implementation make the switchover rather daunting.

The subject of school timings vis-à-vis the sleep pattern of teenagers has yet to trigger a serious debate in our country. In fact, there has been a trend towards opening of high schools earlier than before, while commuting time has been steadily rising in big cities. On top, teenagers are going to bed much later than before, with all their activities late into the night.

The result: many a youngster gets up fighting his biological clock and reaches school carrying a sleep debt. The consequences for students losing sleep by early rising are clear; they lose a significant ability to learn, especially during the beginning teaching periods.

Playing One Parent Against the Other

Raising kids is part joy and part guerrilla warfare

—Ed Asner

Children can be very good at playing one parent off against another.

There are numerous occasions when you find yourself taken by surprise. Your child asks for permission to do something that requires an instant on-the-spot decision, and the spouse is nowhere near.

"Can I have that chocolate bar?" "Can I have a Coke?" "Can I go to the cinema tonight? I need to know quickly as my friend Gopi is on the line and he needs my OK to buy the tickets."

In these cases, you will have to decide one way or the other, and later explain your decision to your partner, especially if the other one has strong views on the subject. You are bound to make the odd slip-up, and you will have to live with the resulting tension with your partner.

There's the other situation where you shift the burden of disciplining an erring kid on to your partner.

"Wait till your father gets home" was the ultimate threat Mummy would make. Or, in these days of dad devaluation, a father warning, "Wait till your mother returns."

It may all seem like an effective tactic—good cop, bad cop. But dumping the burden of discipline for "serious offences" on to the other parent can prove a poor recipe. It just reinforces stereotyped ideas about the different roles of men and women in the family. It makes the father look like an awful tyrant, and rather than making the mother look good, it presents her as being weak. It is like saying, "I don't have the authority or stomach to discipline you." As a result, it eats away all the respect children have for both their mother and father.

Fair discipline is always best administered by the parent who was there when the 'crime' took place. No point dumping your problems on your partner in a situation the other one knows much less about.

Of course, if the offence is serious and you need time to calm down and think before you act, you could say something like, "I and your father will talk about it, and then decide."

A Peep into Parent–Offspring Conflict

We know the scene too well: a boy of four whining loudly in a store when he can't wheedle an extra sweet from his exasperated mother, or a girl of six throwing tantrums at her parents' refusal to buy her a particular doll. Children as young as two or three come to learn that making a public spectacle of their unmet demand can put a lot of pressure on their parents. They often also know that they are safe from parental on-the-spot chastisement in front of others.

Curious as it may sound, such parent–offspring conflicts are not unique to human beings or peculiar to today's children. They are a natural and widely occurring phenomenon in the animal world.

Biologists have found that the animal kingdom abounds with examples of clashes between parents and offspring. And they have developed theories to explain these conflicts. Admittedly, the human scenario is far more complex. Our behaviour is not only dictated by survival strategies that every species adopts, it is also influenced by our social and cultural mores.

According to Robert Travers, a biologist at the University of California, there is an inherent conflict of interests between parents and their offspring in species that reproduce sexually. In such species, each of the two parents contributes exactly half of each offspring's genetic material. Therefore, an offspring is not an exact copy of any parent. And it shares even less than 50 percent genes with its siblings. Because of this genetic differential, each infant has a separate identity and is fully engaged since birth—or even since conception—in single-mindedly pursuing its own interests. And that makes an infant want its parents to lavish all their care on itself, rather than share it out among its siblings. Conflicts arise as the infant struggles to gain maximum parental attention.

Nesting chicks of many birds have been observed raising a frightening ruckus to get maximum foods from their parents, even hurting themselves in the process to gain attention. By their crying and begging and protesting, they want to convey the message that withholding food supplies would have serious consequences on their survival. And chicks wouldn't hesitate to push away other siblings for optimizing their share.

The parent–offspring conflict in the animal world usually works in some sort of a cycle. In the beginning, an offspring often gains the upper hand by impressing parents with its crying and begging. First-time mothers are less immune to such 'deceit' and pressure tactics. In due course, parents get more 'skeptical' and tough-minded. They refuse to administer the amount of care that the infant demands, if it amounts to unfair distribution among the offspring, or places inordinate demands on their capacity or well-being.

Parents are manipulated because they never have perfect knowledge of the needs of the offspring. In reverse, the offspring also does not know how much care the parent is capable of providing. Therefore, the tussle continues until the infant abandons deceit and becomes more truthful about its needs.

Problems sometimes arise in the intervening period when the mother may think that the infant is still crying wolf while the infant is actually truthful.

Budgerigar mothers are known to be quite immune to infant manipulation. They feed their chicks in strict rotation, distributing food in proportion to their age and size. No amount of begging will persuade a budgerigar mother to change this course. In contrast, the male, on the rare occasions he feeds the offspring (he mostly feeds his mate), gives more food to those chicks who beg the loudest and the longest.

So don't be too upset when your child throws a tantrum. It happens all the time in the animal world; it's a part of the game of life. Of course, human children are cleverer. They learn faster and become more skilled at manipulation. How quickly little children learn that most parents will go along than let their children scream in public!

Adolescent Impact on Marital Life

Every family experiences a wave of anxiety when a girl turns twelve or a boy reaches fifteen. As a child enters adolescence, this puts pressure on all aspects of family life, even on the marriage itself.

The anxiety is not necessarily in response to the teenager's overt behaviour; just as often it comes from the parents' fear of the imagined behaviour. What's she actually doing, gone for hours to a friend's house or staying late at a party? How safe is the neighbourhood for her to move about after daylight?

What is the boy doing spending long evenings with his chums? Are they experimenting with drugs? Will he drive his motorbike rashly? Fears extend to accident, death, rape, pregnancy—no small fears.

Even when teenage girls stay demure and well-behaved, anxiety about their potential behaviour is rarely absent.

Parents harbour a brooding awareness of the dangers lurking for the young lives: auto accidents, sexual complications, alcoholic binges, introduction to drugs. They feel panicked by things that adolescents themselves approach in obvious confidence. Indeed, nothing that parents say will dissuade the young from their youthful romps—we all remember ignoring our parents' admonitions.

Parental anxiety is often compounded by the fact that the sight of the teenager revives memories of their own adolescence. And these vivid memories of the thrills experienced and risks encountered add another emotional charge.

Bit by bit, teenage pressure mounts up. In staking claim to his manhood, the boy pushes at the father, who may see the behaviour as insolence or defiance. Surely, the boy needs his father but he also needs to assert his independence.

The father–daughter relationship is no less complex. She wants her father to find her charming, irresistible but totally off-limits. The situation gets more complicated where he is not her biological father.

To the mother, the daughter's growing sexuality often serves as a reminder that her own youth and beauty may well be on the wane.

And then there's the impact of adolescence on marriage itself. It may impel parents to turn to each other with new needs, especially sexual needs, stimulated by the teenager's presence.

Many a couple at this stage is forced to look afresh at their marriage. Is it good or bad? What lies ahead?

Oh, to be young again, to begin life afresh! Not surprisingly, the narcissism of the adolescent is contagious. Some parents get preoccupied with their appearance. Am I too fat? Am I looking old? Am I still attractive?

Yes, all adults do have the wish, consciously or unconsciously, to be the adolescent they are bringing up. We love our children, but at the same time, we envy them. We want them to grow, but we know that it's us they are replacing. Our pride in their achievements mutes our envy, but it does not banish our wish to be young again.

Renu's mother often experiences a tinge of envy when she sees her daughter growing. The girl is growing in a more open, exciting world compared to the traditional one of hers. Kamala had gone from being a protected daughter to a protected wife, and then to a relatively limited life of a homemaker. Even a somewhat inhibited marital sex. In comparison, Kamala sees for Renu all the possibilities of a fuller life.

In a way, a child's adolescence is also a time of parental sadness. We recognize that the teenager is getting emotionally detached, the first step towards his or her eventual separation from us. We lose our special relationship with the child and the feeling of being essential to his or her life.

Parents Versus Peers in the Life of Teenagers

Peers matter much more than parents. Therefore, whatever our parents do to us is overshadowed, in the end, by what our peers do to us.

The above in a nutshell is the argument advanced by grandma Judith Rich Harris in her book *The Nurture Assumption* (1998), a book carrying enthusiastic blurbs from some of the world's top psychologists.

What Harris observes runs counter to nearly everything that a century of psychology has told us about child development. Freud put parents at the centre of the child's universe, and there they have remained ever since. "That's the way I was raised," is quite a common comment, by which we mean that children instinctively and preferentially learn from their parents—parents proving good or bad role models for children. Child development has been, in many ways, concerned with understanding children through their parents.

Since genes account for about half of personality variations among people, parents' contribution in the nature part is obvious. What about the nurture part? The accepted wisdom is that parents mould the personality of their children by doing all the right things—by providing them with every lesson and every experience, by buying them right toys and saying the right words, by helping them in work and games, and by not spanking them or publicly scolding them. The nurture assumption places the credit and blame squarely on parents, in the process turning modern parenthood into a high-responsibility, high-anxiety undertaking. Those who fail to measure up to the strictest standards of supposedly optimal parenting often labour under a sense of guilt. "The frightening thing about heredity and environment is that parents provide both," is quipped.

Harris does not see children as delicate vessels and does not believe they are easily damaged by the missteps of their mothers and fathers. "Kids are not that fragile," she writes. "They are tougher than you think. They have to be, because the world out there does not handle them with kid gloves. At home, they might hear 'What you did made me feel bad' but out on the playground it's 'You shit-head!' "

Observing teenagers around, it began to dawn on Harris that adolescents were wanting to model themselves more on their peers than parents. Children were identifying with and learning from other children. And so came her realization that in a key sense, what's important is not what children learn inside the home but what they learn outside the home.

Harris argues that we have been in the grip of what she calls "nurture assumption", a parent-centred bias that has blinded us to what really matters in human development.

She concludes that while away from parents, children can reconstruct themselves. It is an important limitation on the power of parents. Even when they do succeed in influencing their children, those influences very often don't travel outside the home. And Harris pulls together an extraordinary range of studies and observations in support of the idea.

Just the fact that a child wasn't getting along with his mother didn't necessarily mean that he wouldn't get along with his peers. (Children, after all, are born with individual temperaments. Some children are easy to rear from the start and others are more difficult. And those innate characteristics can strongly influence how parents treat them). In one Swedish study of picky eating among primary-school children cited by Harris, some kids were picky eaters at school, some were picky at home, but only a small number picky at both home and school. A child who pushes away carrots at home might gobble them down in the school cafeteria.

In the same way, a child might stay reserved at home but be a chatterbox in school. In families, the eldest child does seem more serious, responsible and bossy, while the youngest behaves in a more carefree fashion. But outside the home, the younger brother no longer cowed by his older siblings, is perfectly capable of being a dominant, take-charge figure when he's among his friends.

"Socialization research has demonstrated one thing clearly and irrefutably: a parent's behaviour towards a child affects how the child behaves in the presence of the parent or in contexts that are associated with the parent," Harris concludes. "I have no problem with that—I agree with it." But this doesn't necessarily cross into the life a child leads outside the home.

That brings us to one of the Harris's central observations; namely, that kids are not interested in becoming copies of their parents. Children want to be good at being children. How, for example, do you persuade a preschooler to eat something new? Not by eating it yourself and hoping that, your child will follow suit. A preschooler doesn't care what you think. But give the same food to a bunch of preschoolers who like it; it's quite probable that your child will happily follow suit. Children like to wear the kind of clothing other kids are wearing, not the kind their parents are patronizing. From the very moment children meet other children, they take their cues from them. There is a real, strong emotional satisfaction in copying, sharing things. Even for a child of three or four, the group is critical. Ad people know it well; ads targeted at children always show children merrily consuming the advertised product.

Here Harris poses the question: "And, from an evolutionary perspective, who should children be paying attention to? Their parents—the members of the previous generation—or their peers, who will be their future mates and future collaborators? It would be more adaptive to be better tuned to the nuances of their peers' behaviour. That just makes a lot of sense."

That's why neighbourhoods and schools play such a crucial role in the development of a child; a role often as potent as that of home, if not more.

Is Harris right, as she challenges people's cherished ideas about parenthood? She herself admits that what she has provided is only a theory; the same calls for multi-million dollar, multi-year research to back up. Yet she has helped wrench psychology away from its single-minded obsession with parenting—one that sees the development of children almost entirely a story of their parents. To Harris, parents matter but peers seem to matter more.

Devalued Dads

Devaluation of institutions, once seemingly solid and strong, always touches an emotional chord. Here one is not talking of things whose time was up, like our princes, *Rai Bahadurs* or *talukdars*. Governors, judges, even *patwaris* stand devalued. And what about our rupee, once a real rupee?

Yet possibly no one has suffered devaluation as devastating as the dads have. And mind, this species is still relevant; at least biologically if not as much economically.

There was the time before the Second World War when dads were indeed dads. (Why everything had to change with that war?) Even the lowliest babu basked in a bit of royalty when he repaired home after a day's work. Children were hushed and the rowdy ones hid away. Any wordy warfare going on among the inmates of the household abruptly ceased or stood suspended.

Straightaway, he was given something to quench his thirst. And after being duly assisted in his wash-up, the returning hero was soon seated nicely and offered the choicest food his establishment afforded. And he helped himself to his fill without anybody interfering with the process. Dads were known to bang their spoons on the table unless served promptly.

How times have changed?

Now, on seeing Dad enter, the decibel of household noise often goes up, the kids treating him at best as an elder brother more than a boss. Gone are the days when harassed mothers would admonish their errant progeny, "I'll tell your papa when he comes." The situation almost stands reversed. Dads are seen threatening mischief-making brats, "I'll tell your mama."

Teenagers are usually having more loose money on them than their dads. And boys, ravenously hungry, often manage to polish off the best parts of chicken or bulk of the sweet dish before Dad has a chance.

Rarely is he allowed to handle the TV remote or fiddle with the VCR.

There was a time when a boy of 13–14 would fetch the morning milk before he dashed off to school. Now he's probably resting the whole afternoon with blaring music on—after the strenuous labour of dropping a family utility payment in a nearby drop-box. Most of the odd jobs are reserved for Dad.

Traditionally what was good for the dad was good enough for everybody else in the house, whether it was clothes, food, or entertainment. That's a thing of the past. Dad is no longer the model his sons want to be; if anything, they want to be different.

In the consumer culture—which itself is a form of youth culture—the teenager is the king. Advertisers treat him as such.

Once a kid was assumed 'an inferior adult', and he imitated his dad. Now the dad, 'an imperfect adult', is likely to imitate his college-going son in fashion and fads. Consumer culture is not sold on dads.

All in all, the dad's day is nearly done. He is not the captain of the household ship; the passengers have captured the boat. And if he happens to have a working wife, even his breadwinner status stands in serious jeopardy.

How Children React to TV Advertisements?

Whether one likes it or not, our children are coming under increasing exposure to television commercials. Moreover, with the attraction of animation, these ads are the most potent ones for smaller children.

How do children process the advertising message, what do they do with it, and how is their behaviour influenced by what they see and hear? This has become the subject of major research. An attempt is therefore made to summarize their general findings in matters where some common ground has been reached.

Attention to Advertisements

Watching a television commercial for the first time evokes greater attention for the viewer as to what is going on. After several showings, the now familiar commercial, may not receive much attention from the average viewer. However, this does not mean the commercial is not being processed. The system of mental representation that has been activated when the commercial was recognized is driving the processing even when the viewer hears its music from another room.

The attention of very young children, below the age of 3 years, is sporadic. The child rarely sits oriented towards the television set. Later the child starts taking up a position in the room oriented towards the set, playing with toys but also looking up frequently at the television screen. Visual attention to television increases from this time until the age of 5–6.

Younger children tend to pay more attention throughout the commercial—something of intended inertia—compared with older children. Older children's attention within a series of commercials presented in a block tended to drop towards the end.

For all children, full attention to commercials is highest for those advertisements shown at the beginning of programmes. Moreover, for children, the auditory pull of commercials is often more powerful than the visual.

The accustomed viewing style has its impact on attention. For example, viewing in bed, on the floor, at the dining table; or when doing homework or eating or reading comics, or in the presence of friends could result in reduced attention to commercials.

Ability to Distinguish between Advertisements and Programmes

Evidently, it is not difficult to distinguish commercials from rest of the programme. Television commercials are short; programmes are longer. Television ads are repeated in identical form whereas programmes are rarely repeated in the same form. Television commercials are persuasive in intent; programmes can be simply entertaining or informative. And most television programming operates with a recognizable "break" before a commercial interrupts a programme.

It has, however, been observed that a majority of children below six are unable to recognize the difference between commercials and programmes. In fact, the very young are apt to treat people on television like real people, and often wonder where all these people go after the end of a show.

An ability to distinguish between commercials and programmes is reckoned as a crucial factor in building a child's defences against ads.

Understanding the Intent of Commercials

What are television commercials? What do they try to do? If children of different ages are asked questions like these, their replies commonly vary according to their ages. Older children aged nine or over might say that they are there to persuade you buy things. Children of 5–6 may simply say ads are fun, and they are there to make you laugh. To some children of 7–8, ads could be telling important things.

In one experiment, half of the 11-year-olds interviewed felt that commercials do not always tell the truth. As children grow up, they start conceiving the character of TV commercials as more persuasive than assistive. Children of parents with higher educational levels will tend to attribute persuasive intent at an earlier age—by 10 or so—than the children of parents with lower educational levels.

To most experts, the attribution of persuasive intent is a vital component when processing advertising messages. Being able to conceive of this purpose behind commercials leads to "cognitive defences" against advertising.

The Child's Memory of Commercials

There is a major change in the type of information recalled from commercials. Younger children tend to recall single elements while older children tend to remember more of the plot and the product advertised.

The Effects of Advertising

It is possible to 'arm' children against commercials (more so against the press of sugared products) and to use consumer educational strategies to reduce their vulnerability to commercial appeal. Also, the two most vulnerable groups (heavy viewers and young children) appear to be the ones on whom consumer education can work best.

The general research consensus is that children's attitudes to television commercials tend to become more negative as they grow older. Some older children even find ads silly. Of course, some commercials are intrinsically more interesting than others are, and this will influence the extent to which children want to watch a particular commercial.

Older children and adolescents, in order to distance themselves from younger children, often claim to be unimpressed and cynical about ads. Heavy viewers, however, tend to like and trust commercials and express stronger behavioural intentions towards products advertised.

Researchers have not been able to evolve any consensus about the eventual effects of advertising on children's behaviour, though they deem it a matter of crucial importance. At the most, they make out that there is a short-term increase in the demand and consumption of sugared products because of advertisement, especially of the brands heavily advertised.

There is an emerging agreement among experts that controls on television commercials primarily targeted at children need some tightening. For example, care has to be taken that television commercials don't make appeals which contend that if children have a product they are better than their peers or lacking it will not be accepted by their peers. The child's feelings and motives must not be manipulated—easier said than enforced. Many countries debar the use of cartoon characters to endorse products. France and Denmark go further and do not allow anyone under 12 to endorse products. The idea behind this restriction is that someone below 12 is not really in a position to judge the suitability of an advertised product. A few countries have now started insisting on a health warning in confectionery commercials. All in all some clear ground rules have to be enforced, especially when advertisers have every incentive to exploit loopholes in their bid for aggressive selling.

We have ads where a kid of seven or eight is seen endorsing a particular motor bike. He is often shown on the saddle itself. Evidently, there is a good case for controlling such inept ads.

The Magic of the Family Meal

Eating together offers an ideal opportunity for a family to communicate, to interact. Indeed, without a family meal to bring everyone together, there is no other forum of communication, no other focus to family life, no domestic debating chamber, no medium for the exchange of wisdom between the different generations.

Yet the custom of a family eating together has been steadily fading in several societies. For example, a majority of the British and Americans have given up eating together. In many homes, nobody even cooks on a regular basis. Anybody feeling hungry approaches the fridge and fashions a meal for himself, or brings along some carry-home stuff. No fixed timings of meals, no fixed place to eat. Each member of the household develops a separate life, fitting eating into his or her own work-cum-recreation schedule. In quite a few families, the only mode of communication between teenagers and their parents is now through slips pasted on the fridge door.

Others, such as the Italians, are still mostly keeping to the custom of a family sitting down to a meal, once a day or at least several times a week, while the housewife cooks. Children learn how to manage a knife and fork, how to behave, how to talk.

In this respect, we are more like the Italians. Yet in many an urban, upwardly mobile home, the Anglo–American pattern seems to be setting in. Children tend to eat in their rooms in the midst of their activities and at their own time. In fact, one gets an impression that many a teenager is at pains to avoid any talk with parents—keeping such conversation limited to grunts and shrugs.

The family meal, primarily the evening meal, is not only the core curriculum in the school of civilized discourse. It is also a set of protocols that curb our natural savagery and animal greed. It cultivates in us a capacity for sharing and considerateness for others. Indeed, table manners are one of the subtlest lines separating civility from barbarity.

Dinner rituals have little to do with the income or the social class of a family. It is not important whether you sit at a big dining table or squat on the kitchen floor. And you could have the simplest food imaginable; plain dal and roti would do.

What really counts is the grace with which food is served and accepted. It is through this practice of the family sitting at meals and observing the attendant conventions that youngsters learn the art of human companionship, the culture of give and take.

Moreover, the ideal family meal calls for undistracted dining, not sitting in front of the TV. Even otherwise, new research shows that families who watch TV during dinnertime tend to develop poor eating habits, putting kids at risk from obesity or malnutrition. A Tufts University study, released by the American Academy of Pediatrics, found that when families didn't separate eating from other activities, particularly watching TV, kids consumed fewer fruits and vegetables and more junk food. Left to their own devices, youngsters almost inevitably gravitate to fast food, hardly brimming with nutrients.

In one recent study of 5,000 families published in the *Journal of the American Dietic Association,* frequent family meals signified an increasing intake of healthy foods.

Another study published in the *Journal of Adolescent Health* also found that eating evening meals at home was associated with an increased consumption of fruits and vegetables, and healthier eating habits overall.

The more frequent family dinners are, the more likely the youngsters are to discuss and learn about nutritional matters.

Eating is one of the most fundamental health-related behaviour we have. Cutting out distractions at mealtimes, such as TV, is the best way to ensure that healthier foods make it to the table. Once parents manage to separate and structure eating times, incorporating healthy foods becomes much simpler.

A factor undermining the institution of the family meal is the spreading habit of "grazing". People, particularly teenagers, keep on taking snacks at all hours or snatching food whenever convenient. This does erode the imperative of a regular, fixed-time sit-down meal.

Teenagers gulping junk food slouched in front of TV or snacking at odd hours cooped up in their rooms, are not only be nutritionally deprived, they are deprived of the best element of family life; the family meal. It would be an error to underestimate its importance in the character formation of the young.

Well, their parents can also be faulted for this development. These parents—mostly working parents—may be too busy in their business deals or social whirl. Or, they may simply be preferring nice, quiet meals. Eating with youngsters entails enforcing a modicum of discipline and smoothening individual behaviour. That way all rituals involve some degree of sacrifice in time and attention. And the same is true of the sit-together family meal.

"The family that prays together stays together," said Al Scalpone. It could well be said that the family that eats together stays together.

Picky Eating

A 4-year-old throwing tantrums when faced with any unfamiliar food—unless it's sweet. This dinner-table scenario exasperates many a parent.

Taste researchers theorize that 4-year-olds become picky as a survival strategy. At that age, they are old enough to find food on their own, but not old enough to judge what is safe to eat and what is not. An ingrained fear of new foods protects a child from poisoning.

Picky eating can be quite annoying to parents. Yet this behaviour should be taken more as a temporary inconvenience than any serious problem.

Other researchers have shown that forcing kids to swallow an unappealing vegetable, before being allowed to eat the pudding, could simply make a kid hate that vegetable more as well as love the pudding more.

Surveys have shown that it takes something like ten experiences with a new food for a kid to learn to like it.

We are hardwired to prefer the sweet and avoid the bitter. Humans are born loving sweetness. On its very first day, a newborn prefers sweetened drinks to bland ones. Bitterness is a sign of toxicity. No wonder the human tongue comes equipped with an elaborate bitter alarm system.

Our proclivities to food are shaped at a very early age. Biologists contend that the flavours we sample while in the womb itself, stay with us into infancy and perhaps well beyond. Experiments showed that if a woman took orange juice regularly during pregnancy, her baby is apt to like orange-flavoured drinks when no more than six months old. Nursing babies also seem to detect flavours like vanilla in their mother's milk. Breast-fed babies of mothers who ate a wide range of foods are more likely to embrace new foods later on. That way, mother's milk is one of the first ways babies learn.

Being picky in food is not a phenomenon restricted to children. Mild pickiness is widespread among adults. For example, many adults do not like slippery food like oysters or okra. Others avoid stuffed things like egg rolls or stuffed potatoes. Some people do not like the gooeyness inside tomatoes. Many prefer their breakfast to stay unvaried, eating the same stuff day after day, month after month, year after year.

Teenagers Driving

Recent studies of fatal road crashes by teenage drivers have thrown up a few revealing findings. According to these, a teenager driving solo is safer. A teenager driving with one teen passenger doubles the fatal crash risk. With more than two teenage passengers, the fatal crash risk is almost five times as high as driving alone. And gender matters: the highest-risk situation is with male teenagers. (Having passengers or not has no effect on safety with older drivers.)

The biggest reason for fatal teen accidents has been shown to be inexperience and immaturity. Teenager drivers tend to get themselves into situations they can't recover from. New drivers make mistakes such as overcorrecting at a corner or slamming too hard on brakes and skidding.

Consequently, several countries are putting restrictions on teenager driving. One favoured approach is to issue a provisional driving permit at the age of 16. The provisional licence—commonly valid for six months in the first instance—restricts teenage passengers and late-night driving. And the permit is suspended if the teen has an accident, commits a driving violation (as minor as not wearing a seatbelt), or is caught driving after drinking even a trace of alcohol.

Of course, it is not as much fun driving with parents as with one's friends, yet teenagers are being advised to undergo a certain amount of supervised driving, just to get a feel for judging distances and speeds.

The usual scenario for accidents: youngsters driving in the company of friends, often after a drinking session. And speeding on the city's wide roads that are invitingly empty in the wee hours of the night. These are single-vehicle accidents and severe.

The youngsters' company encourages speeding, even an element of daredevilry, combined with a young driver's lack of driving experience. And further, there is the young driver's inability to handle alcohol compared to older adults who are habituated to it over years of drinking.

Moderating teenage driving through licence control may not be very effective in our conditions. A lot of teenagers are known to be driving without a licence, often within the knowledge of their parents. And our system of issuing driving licences itself stays far too lax to assure driving competency.

Consequently, we have to rely more on education. Educating parents about the risks of unsupervised driving at the stage when the teens are immature and inexperienced. And educating teenagers about the added risks they run in driving with buddies as passengers, and worse still, driving under the influence of alcohol.

6

Married Couples Living in Joint Family

More and more couples, particularly middle-class couples in cities, are opting for living as a nuclear family, along with their children. However, a large number of married couples are still living in joint families—with parents, brothers, sisters and some other close relations.

Mother-in-Law/Daughter-in-Law Relationships

At Unisinos, a university in Sao Leopoldo, Brazil, courses have been developed on mother-in-law/daughter-in-law conflict. There they analyse what can go wrong and what can be done to set it right.

The standard 15-hour course with 40 participants (mothers-in-law and daughters-in-law roughly equal in number) is proving popular. Dr Fetter, the course director, when asked whether there was any tension among participants, said jokingly, "The only fighting that goes on is to find a place in the course." The course for women is so successful, the university is planning a similar one for male in-laws. Possibly, we also need similar course(s) in some of our universities and allied institutions.

In cultures all over the world, mothers-in-law—with their No-One-Is-Good-Enough-for-My-Boy belief—have a dodgy reputation. In Italy, for example, the Supreme Court has ruled that being forced to live with a mother-in-law is a ground for a woman to ask for divorce. A plant with long, sharp-edged leaves has been given the name of 'mother-in-law's tongue.' The phenomenon of mother-in-law and daughter-in-law living together continues to remain more of a common occurrence in India than in the West.

This adverse image, however, is gradually undergoing a change. Previously it was always a live-in mother-in-law. Now, more often, it's a visiting mother-in-law. Anyway the mother-in-law jokes are no longer in favour.

Admittedly, the mother-in-law/daughter-in-law relationship is far more complex and sensitive than, say, of mother and daughter. A mother and daughter can be forthright with each other, even be furious with each other—and then make up. Any confrontation between a mother-in-law and daughter-in-law is rarely such a simple, straightforward affair.

To a daughter-in-law the initial reception from her mother-in-law is rather crucial (a point whose importance some mothers-in-law underestimate, with the hope of making amends later on). If she isn't made to feel welcome, the younger woman may take it as being found wanting. This perceived rebuff may affect her relationship with her mother-in-law for a long time, even leave permanent scars. And it comes harder to a daughter-in-law whose background occupies a lower rung on the socio-economic ladder.

Where a daughter-in-law's socio-economic background is well above that of her mother-in-law, differences in lifestyle could add stress on both sides, particularly if the newcomer tries to wean her husband away from the customs of the family. The in-laws may feel rejected.

To have a daughterless mother-in-law can well be a disadvantage. A daughterless mother-in-law may not know how to relate to a younger woman. Or, she may hope that her daughter-in-law will be the dreamed-of perfect daughter she never had.

Various surveys reveal that the younger the mother-in-law, the better the relationship between the two women. And, where both of them work, full time or part-time, their relationship gets an added plus. Working mothers-in-law and daughters-in-law know what it means to juggle a job, home and children. Even mothers-in-law who have retired but worked once, display a greater tendency of non-interference with their children's lives. And, of course, where the live-in mother-in-law is there to share the housekeeping and childcare burden of the working housewife, she's doubly welcome. As childcare goes there could be no better care-takers than mothers-in-law to their grandchildren.

What often causes maximum trouble between a mother-in-law and daughter-in-law is the rendering of "advice" by the senior woman, the younger woman interpreting it as criticism. Many a mother-in-law sincerely believes she gives advice only when necessary. But who's to judge what's 'necessary'? Actually, a certain amount of advice-giving is a part of our daily conversations; we all dole it out to others, and a mother-in-law is no exception to this condition. But such advice can only be tolerated in small doses, with the tone and manner of handing it out being just right. Otherwise it puts the young daughter-in-law, still unsure of herself, on the defensive. Once she has matured and acquired the necessary self-confidence, she can cope much better with the advice coming from the senior woman, even appreciating it.

Ideally, a 'good' mother-in-law ought not to make critical remarks about the way her grandchildren are brought up—that's primarily the responsibility of parents. But this is easier said than done. At certain moments, a mother-in-law may be unable to control her accumulated feelings about what she believes good or bad for a child, and blurt out her suggestions. This is commonly construed by a daughter-in-law as meddling in the upbringing of children—in things like whether the baby be left to cry or be picked up, the strict enforcement of bedtime, the amount of TV viewing to be allowed, and so on. Grandparents are often charged with 'spoiling' grandchildren with their indulgent approach.

For a mother-in-law, it is wise and helpful to think of her son and his wife as a couple from the very beginning. Any serious discussion with her son over family matters should include the daughter-in-law.

The wife who can think of her mother-in-law as her husband's mother, instead of associating her with the stereotyped mother-in-law of myths and jokes, will be starting off well. Her husband may occasionally complain of his mother, but if the wife joins him in attacking the mother, he'll eventually come to resent it.

One of the deepest gratification of a mother-in-law is to feel wanted and needed. It's therefore a good strategy for a daughter-in-law to keep on asking for her help or advice in day-to-day matters. And a widowed mother-in-law is to be extended greater consideration; widowhood magnifies the need for feeling wanted, more so if she lacks other satisfactions such as work, friends or hobbies.

By and large, with the education and advancement of women, coupled with a growing democratisation of our family life, the relationship between mothers-in-law and daughters-in-law is assuming a more sophisticated, appreciative shape. Still the longest war in history, one that ruined many a marriage, is far from over. Anything that helps defuse the tension is welcome. And, in this context, the sort of courses started by the Brazilian university are a help.

Back into the Empty Nest

Another facet of the empty nest problem is that the children who fly abroad for education or training, unlike those who may go only out of town, most often do not return. They become NRIs in the US, UK, Australia and several other countries. Here, the aged couples are perpetually missing the company of their children gone away. At best, it is an annual visit for them to visit their children settled abroad or the children visiting India.

Sudha, a Delhiite, married a software programmer in Bangalore and left for that city. After five years, her husband opened his own consultancy firm in Delhi. She moved back into the empty parental nest—a big four-bedroom house in Vasant Vihar with her husband and a boy of three.

Originally, it was for want of readily available accommodation. Now Sudha's family is so well adjusted living there, she runs the kitchen in lieu of rent. The ageing parents—their son stays in the USA—now live like guests in their own home.

Raman is a dentist. He lived with his parents in Panchsheel, Delhi, the father a retired chief engineer. Raman married a dentist. They moved to a flat in Safdarjung Enclave but found it hard to run a comfortable home within the constraints of their newly started practice. So when Rani got pregnant, they moved back to his parents.

With both Raman and Rani busy in their dental clinic, the two small girls, twins, are mostly left in the care of grandparents. The Ramans—who have started contributing a fixed sum of Rs. 20,000 per month towards house running—have the use of a first-rate accommodation, unequalled daycare-givers for their kids, and nice hot meals on return from work. Rani is quite reconciled to a stray sarcastic remark from her mother-in-law as long as the cozy arrangement persists.

Unmarried sons and daughters, even in their late twenties or early thirties, mostly continue to stay with their parents. To these older children, living at home seems far nicer and much more comfortable.

Parents, particularly parents in Delhi, seem to be subjected to a peculiar phenomenon. Their sons who moved out on marriage often want to return to the "empty nest". This means living rent-free and subsidized, with no scheduled date for departure. Sometimes even a married daughter returns, not necessarily a divorcee, but with her hubby and children in tow. Again, grown-up sons and daughters are showing a marked preference to staying on in the parental home than seeking lodgings elsewhere.

Cynics say, it is not a resurgence of filial affection; it's the city's housing shortage and soaring rents that is forcing the trend.

Another or an added reason is advanced like this. Many young couples are now working couples; it is becoming increasingly difficult to sustain an urban middle-class lifestyle on a single income, let alone the women's desire to be engaged in satisfying work.

Once young wives used to harbour a horror of joint-family living, and were often instrumental in setting up separate establishments. Now when she has kids and a full-time job, the advantages of joint-family living loom larger than its drawbacks in reduced privacy and occasional unpleasantness (the proverbial nastiness between mothers-in-law and daughters-in-law is clearly on the decline).

You get babysitters gratis. And what babysitters! You can't match grandparents in the quality of their caring, and availability on tap. When you come home tired from work, you have things tidied up and a hot meal cooking.

In the West, particularly the USA, leaving one's home on reaching adulthood was deemed something normal, almost taken for granted. Let alone the boys and girls, the parents themselves were insistent about it. Of late, there has been a perceptible change there, too. With inflated rents and job insecurity, young adults are returning home in increasing numbers. And parents have grown generally indulgent in receiving them back.

So far, so good, for the children.

What about the parents, turned into permanent parents? Is it a rewarding experience for them to play the extended host? Or, does it usually turn out to be a tiresome affair?

It is hard to generalize in such matters; the range of possibilities is enormous. A great deal depends on personal equation, and on the personalities of the players involved, with the role of the daughter-in-law as crucial. Factors like family finances and the space available are important.

However, one can venture a few general observations in this minefield of human relationships.

Where the parents, especially the father in his sixties, is active and working, he could well see his thirty-year-old live-in more as a 'buddy' than father and son. The two may be dressing the same way, going to the same clubs, or playing, say, golf together. Or a vivacious daughter of twenty-eight making the parental house lively with her presence. Today's twenty-something and their modern parents communicate better and closer. And people tend to prize the closeness of family relationships.

When the nest is doubly empty, one parent having died, the surviving one often pines for close relationships with children as a surviving widow. But then widows in their 50s or 60s can make a mistake in getting too involved with their adult children. They have decades ahead and need to find a way to approach their lives as individuals.

Parents like being in a position to help their kids financially or otherwise, and they like the fact that they get along well enough to live together. But parents do suffer potential emotional repercussions. The empty-nest years are a crucial time for them to bone up on retirement rather than feed their adult children. Keeping the kids also prevents couples from reconfiguring their lives in the post-parenting stage.

Having an adult child lurking around the house and feeding off of the parental nest egg robs parents of some of this latitude. Experts tend to agree that having an adult kid at home is generally a bad idea. *How to Survive and Thrive in an Empty Nest: Reclaiming Your Life When Your Children Have Grown* by Robert Lauer and Jeanette Lauer (Counterpoint Press) dwells on this theme.

Anyway, everyone must understand his or her role when living together. Some parents, especially mothers, make the mistake of imagining that their adult children are still somewhat helpless. Adult children have to be treated as adults with adult responsibilities and obligations. Whether adults age 25 or 45, these children should shoulder their share of household tasks. They can't expect everything to be just as it was before—with the mother saddled with the bulk of work. Many parents who have re-nesting children get frustrated, because they feel slaves to their children.

This becomes particularly galling to parents who were looking forward to their "empty nest" years—these years getting longer with the lengthening life spans—for a relaxed life of peace and quiet, with time enough for each other and for pursuing their interests. Instead, they find themselves landed up with the same tensions and problems they had encountered at the child-raising stage. The cooking remains more elaborate, and the house is disorderly.

Besides sharing fully in household tasks, the re-nesting children must regularly pay the agreed rent. Pay it regularly and unobtrusively, such as by an automatic bank transfer every month. Face-to-face payments are not only embarrassing, these often tend to fall in arrears or get 'forgotten'. And, one assumes, other expenses would be shared suitably.

Parents' privacy has to be respected zealously. Older people are a little more anxious to keep their love life secret, and their love life may be more active than you imagine.

You can't always buy peace by shoving your rowdy kids into an older couple's rest periods. One's grandchildren can be great fun but only if the fare is served in controlled measure.

All in all, re-nesting children should not make their parents feel as if they were being taken advantage of.

How Good are Grandparents?

> "The entrance requirements for grandpahood are comparatively mild, you only have to live until your child has a child."
>
> —Ogden Nash,

Grandparents are people who come to your house, spoil the children, and then go home. Children, especially smaller children, are mainly interested in the presents grandparents bring. These are generally more expensive, more elaborate presents. Indeed, some toy shops have a special Grandma's Corner where more expensive gift items are exhibited.

The significance of grandparenthood evokes much interest and speculation. Yet it is backed by scant verification and research.

Grandparents themselves seem unable to speak of their role in anything but laudatory terms. Most speak glowingly of the joys of grandparenthood, particularly of the fun with those adorable, small grandchildren. That way, "Nothing makes a boy smarter than being a grandson".

In the process, grandparents may indulge their grandchildren in a way parents cannot; in fact, in ways parents may not approve. Yet this is a relationship from which grandparents derive much satisfaction. Indeed, nothing is harder on a grandparent than having to watch a grandchild being disciplined.

It is sometimes made out that such indulgence from grandparents served a salutary purpose for the grandchildren, as it functioned as a relief from the tensions caused between the parents and children by parental authority. Yet, modern parents themselves are becoming permissive these days, and usually adopt an egalitarian and friendly relationship with their children. Hence, children do not need grandparents as mediators or allies against parental authority.

Many a sociologist has come to believe that in modern times, grandparenthood is a largely 'inactive' role that does not bring continuing interaction into the lives of grandparents. They are just permitted to dispense certain services and material support, and to engage in certain expressive activities, yet mostly prohibited from encroaching upon the parental responsibilities of their adult children or interfere with their authority.

These sociologists attribute this downsizing of grandparental role to the high value being placed upon the independence of the nuclear family in child rearing. Their writings create an image of grandparents as 'meddlesome intruders' in family processes. The once favoured position of the grandfather and grandmother is being undermined.

Others make out that grandparents live on the fringe of a nuclear family, so long as the family remains intact. However, in the event of a breakup or the death of a spouse, grandparents assume a vital function, providing a source of rescue or refuge for grandchildren. And grandmothers often take on major household responsibilities when the mother is working or giving birth, and lend assistance in times of illness or crisis. Even economic help is sometimes given in the form of shared living arrangements. The flow of aid, particularly financial aid, is chiefly from the parents to the children, especially in the early years of the latter's marriage.

That way, despite a decrease in joint family living, middle-class parents and their married children usually do develop a regular pattern of mutual aid in nursing care, festivities and other activities.

Where young married middle-class couples deem it important to avoid obligations and keep their independence, their parents find indirect ways of helping their married children. The most common method is to give substantial gifts to their grandchildren.

What's the significance of grandparenthood to grandchildren? Very few investigators have examined the grandparent–grandchild relationship, often called a 'magical' relationship.

One interesting thing revealed in studies is that young people with grandparents and great-grandparents have fewer age prejudices than those who do not. When the grandchild sees his grandfather organizing his life with meaning and purpose, the former entertains not only a certain pride in owning up the latter, but also actively indulges in even exaggerating grandpa's busy schedule.

Studies also show that grandparents have different significance for children at different development ages (4–5, 8–9, and 11–12). The youngest group valued grandparents mainly for their indulgent qualities; the middle group preferred active, fun-sharing grandparents, and the oldest group appeared to have become distant from their grandparents.

The changing status of grandparents, and the influence this will have on the grandparent–grandchild relationship, should be an area of emerging interest in family research.

Most grandparents appear to find the grandparent role comfortable and pleasant; have all the fun and none of the responsibility. They don't hold themselves accountable for the mistakes or shortcomings of their grandchildren, but like to bask in the reflected glory when grandchildren achieve success.

A person who wishes to become a valued grandparent should learn to accept change, and should be able to relinquish the parent role with his children and enter into a new role with his grandchildren, a role that supplements the parental role and in no way conflicts or competes with it.

It is still to be established whether grandparents influence their grandchildren directly, or whether their influence is largely indirect (through their children in the middle generation). And here, again, tension in relations with one's adult children may often prevent a satisfactory relationship from developing between grandparents and grandchildren.

Grandparenthood is one of the few 'ready-made' roles available to the ageing person at a point in his life when his former roles are lost or decrease in significance: "A man begins to show his age about the same time he begins to carry pictures of his grandchildren".

When an individual retires or is widowed or exits from other roles, grandparenthood begins to assume greater importance for him. Surely grandparents look for every opportunity to play host to their grandchildren. But then small children with their pranks and noise can prove quite tiring to elderly grandparents.

Nowadays, however, many people become grandparents when they are relatively young (men in fifties, women in forties) and active in their jobs. With the longevity trend, grandparenthood has become a middle-age rather than an old-age phenomenon.

At the middle-age stage, grandparents are often not in a position to give the desired time and attention to their small grandchildren. In later years, when major roles are gone and they have plenty of time for grandchildren, this role may have lost its salience. With grandchildren grown up into adolescence or adulthood, the opportunity to develop a meaningful relationship or even enjoying their company may have elapsed.

Roles Reversed

"Careful. Keep a hand on the railing, negotiating stairs," I say to my father. And insist, "he has an escort when taking a walk in the adjoining park. At the table, we heap food on his plate, instead of letting him help himself. I even dish out advice on how he should conduct himself in the bathroom without risking a fall."

The lively eighty-five-year old, a widower for six months, is visiting us for the winter. In fact, he was not keen on stirring out of his Chandigarh home but for my going there to fetch him.

Here is a man who was once the most commanding figure in my boyhood, an overpowering presence. I used to hang on to every word of his. He taught me how to handle a shotgun and knot a necktie. Tall and muscular, he was strong enough to fight off a robber or beat the hell out of a street bully, so I imagined. When he was annoyed, the whole household shivered. Indeed, all quarrels and loud voices stood suspended when he was sighted coming.

As the headmaster of a prestigious high school for twenty years, his standing with students was something special. He was both feared and respected. Whenever seen approaching, boys would sound an alert, "Hark, the headmaster". This put everybody on his best behaviour.

Parenting is said to be an invigorating experience. It is a good deal of fun too, despite its quota of conflicts and problems. However, 'parenting' one's parent is rarely a smooth affair. The role reversal, a truly complex phenomenon, is never free from an element of frustration and embarrassment.

Is it so because it goes against nature's very scheme of things? In the animal world, the old are not parented by their offspring.

The elderly parent, more so a widower, is often anxious to retain a measure of independence, or at least a semblance of it. Physical assistance is accepted but with a marked preference for the unobtrusive variety, not the showy sort. Old men tend to be touchy about it; they do not want their physical infirmities to be advertised.

The elderly parent again wants to preserve his or her lifestyle to the extent feasible. No wonder my father feels far more comfortable in his own modest home than as a guest at a more affluent one.

The elderly again mostly wish to be no burden to their progeny, as long as one is not disabled. Of course, one has to be in possession of ready cash or property. The lot of a penniless parent is rarely free of humiliations.

The dilemmas of those parenting a parent perhaps lie even deeper. Whatever he or she does, it never seems to be enough. One always ends up feeling a bit guilty. A dutiful daughter with an old, infirm mother on her hands can harbour an uncomfortable feeling, she is not discharging her obligations well—no matter however irritatingly the mother might have treated her as a girl. Many a mother in senility is known to revert to a petulant, demanding toddlerhood.

The task of parenting the parent becomes more daunting for the only child. And it can give rise to a sense of frustration, as the parent is often emotionally more demanding. At times, previously unresolved conflicts have a way of surfacing.

An elderly single parent, independent, well-off, and enjoying 'the good life' is now an increasing possibility. Yet numerous parents cannot escape a state of dependence on their middle-aged children—a state that could turn out to be an embarrassment to the elderly and irksome to the parenting children.

This role-reversal is not such an easy thing to manage.

7

Healthcare in Marriage

Men and Women in Matters of Health

Being a man can be damaging to your health. Under the age of 50, men are more at risk of heart disease than women, the latter partially protected by the estrogen they produce until they reach menopause. Women have more durable hearts. With men, heart-related mortality rates soar after thirty-five, while women's heart problems don't usually crop up till forty-five.

Men's testosterone causes increased levels of bad cholesterol in their blood and suppresses the good kind, whereas in women, estrogen has precisely the opposite effect.

Throughout their lives, women have stronger immune systems than men, thanks to a higher number of T-cells.

Women have slower metabolism than men, which may mean that men's cells are placed under greater stress throughout life, or, put simply, that their life cycle completes itself sooner. No wonder, in societies where females suffer no discrimination in food or health care vis-à-vis males, women on average live longer by 4–5 years.

Women are less prone to cancers of the lung, bladder and the stomach, but more susceptible to such chronic conditions as arthritis and osteoporosis.

Women have better hearing and sense of smell—evidently, nature wanting them to respond quicker to their baby's cries and smells. Women's memory functions better and longer into old age as compared to men.

And because women have less testosterone that contributes to baldness, they are less likely to lose their hair.

Men have a higher incidence of myopia, hernia, acne, and flatulence than women. And are heir to more genetic disorders such as colour blindness or left-handedness.

On top, men are natural exuberant risk takers, loving dangerous sports, binge drinking, and being sexually more predatory.

Men tend to take more chances with their health. And when things go wrong, are less inclined to do anything about it, much less consult a doctor. On average, men go to doctors half as many times as women. Indeed, many men visit doctors only when their wives make them do so.

Even when it becomes imperative to see a doctor, men often don't do it properly. It could mean skipping on the case history or otherwise belittling the problem—both male patients and male doctors have absorbed lessons in being strong and silent. One survey of the UK's National Health Service revealed that a consultation between a woman GP and a woman patient will last four times as long as one between a male doctor and a male patient.

If women risk cancer of the breast and ovaries, men equally risk prostate cancer, let alone problems with urination from an enlarged prostate.

Happily, in recent years, an increasing awareness of men's health problems is emerging. It is also being realized that improving men's health will improve women's health, too. After all, women suffer looking after their sick men folk.

Finally, what's the secret to a long-lasting sexual relationship in marriage? Here, Dr Joyce Brothers has this to offer to men as her best advice: "The secret is keeping yourself clean and attractive in terms of grooming. I'm talking about bathing and shaving and all those things. And telling the other person how terrific they are."

Husbands Who Neglect Their Health

What should a wife do when she sees her husband neglecting his health? This is the predicament of Reena, a trim forty-eight. Her husband, fifty-four, drinks, smokes, overeats and does no regular exercise. He even skips the nightly teeth brushing, content with rinsing his mouth with water. Little wonder he is developing a pronounced paunch.

Mohan Misra, a senior bank manager, takes immense care about the health of his bank. And he is otherwise well-informed, well-read. But when it comes to taking care of his own health, to his wife he seems quite remiss.

When she tells Mohan to quit smoking or restrict his alcohol intake to no more than two whiskies in an evening, or heap smaller helpings of dessert on his plate, he takes it more as nagging than friendly advice. "I'm healthy for my 54 years. Why should I change my lifestyle? Why lower the quality of my life for some fancy health fads?" he says. "Anyway, we have long lives in our family; you know papa is going strong at 85."

Yes, Mohan is all right at 54. But will he be healthy at 60 or 65? That's what Reena can't help worrying about.

And she is not alone in such worries. Countless wives of smokers, drinkers, overeaters and under-exercisers ask the same question. Why do blokes, otherwise smart and successful, behave so dumb when it comes to taking care of their own health?

One possible explanation lays in the differing perceptions men and women have about their bodies. Men are brought up to take risks—it's the macho thing to take risks—and that includes taking risks with one's own body. Men by nature are exuberant creatures: loving dangerous sports, drinking heavily, driving fast.

A new book *The Adonis Complex* (Simon & Schuster) by three of the world's leading authorities in psychiatry—Harvard's Harrison Pope and Dr. Robert Olivardia, and Professor Katharine Phillips of Brown University—has pulled together all the evidence from a multitude of studies to make an irrefutable case highlighting the dangerous relationship between men and their bodies and the impact this has on their marital relationships.

Admittedly, compared to the female body, the male one is a low-maintenance proposition: trim the finger nails every 10 days, a haircut once a month, and that daily chore of shaving. A man's body does not betray its tenant as rapidly as a woman's. Never as fine and lovely, it has had less distance to fall. "The male body skims the surface of nature's deeps, where the blood and pain and mysterious cravings of women perpetuate the species. Participating less than the female body in nature's processes, the male body gives the impression of being exempt from time," says John Updike, the noted novelist.

Again men aren't that concerned as to how they look (admittedly the same could be fast changing with trendy young males). A few pounds of flab on the belly do not bother many a man. In fact, when they look in the mirror, men, unlike women, generally like what they see and feel no serious compulsion to take cumbersome remedial measures. Being less critical, men have a whole lot less motivation to change their ways, with far fewer worry about their weight as compared to women.

What's a wife supposed to do when she feels convinced her hubby hasn't been taking good care of himself? Doing nothing about it would virtually amount to colluding with him. And yet her pointing this out has to be tactful, not to be construed as nagging. A bit of humour in the telling always helps.

Possibly her most effective strategy is to set an example. She can take to indoor exercise or vigorous walks/jogging. Chances are he would join at some stage. And she could cut down the calories in home cooking. Here she will do well to take him into confidence, lest he undo all her good work by gorging on sweets and snacks outside.

And if still he continues blithely negligent about his health, she better persuade him to take a higher life insurance policy.

Taking Your Medicine

It is estimated that half of all patients who take medicines do not take them right. They either eat the wrong foods with their medication, or happen to mix their medicines with alcohol intake, or take them at the wrong time. According to Dorothy Smith, an American researcher on the subject, around 30 percent of patients could be jeopardizing their health through mistakes in administering their medicines.

Here are a few suggestions to minimize chances of such errors.

You should clearly know the name of the drug you're taking, its dosage, and what foods and drinks you should avoid taking with it. And so also foods which could make the medicine more effective.

As to what to drink to wash down the pill, water is nearly always a good choice. Fruit juices can destroy certain drugs before they reach your blood stream. Even milk can render a few drugs ineffective, like tetracycline. On the other hand, milk is recommended for some medication because it settles the stomach.

Taking pills with coffee or tea can present problems as both these beverages contain caffeine. So better, consult your doctor whether caffeine would adversely influence your medicine.

When you take a pill, resist the common tendency to throw your head back as you put the pills on your tongue, followed by a gulp of water. The pill will naturally rise to the back of your mouth and go down more easily.

If you're in bed when you take a pill, don't lie down again for a minute or two after you've swallowed it, to be sure it has gone all the way down.

Quite a few books are now available that give information to consumers about common drugs in layman's language—things like the generic and brand names, usual dosages and other characteristics. If you or your family members are a regular consumer of medicines, it's worthwhile to become more familiar with your medicines through reference to such publications. Dorothy Smith's book *Understanding Prescription Drugs* falls in this category, listing more than 800 drugs. It has illustrations how to administer them, and a host of other useful information about taking medicines.

Tired All the Time

"It is part of the cure to wish to be cured."

—Seneca, the Roman sage

"I am doing everything right. I eat well. I sleep well. I exercise. I don't smoke or drink. Why am I tired all the time? Why, why, why?" asks Prema's husband from their family doctor in exasperation.

Yes, her husband, Randhir, has every right to ask that question.

The Chronic Fatigue Syndrome (CFS) is the commonest urban malady. And it's more common in the age group 25 to 40—otherwise, a healthy phase of life. Indeed, CFS is said to be higher in women than men. Around three-fourth of CFS patients are found to suffer from some sort of depression.

CFS poses a puzzle to doctors. It has no identified cause and no specific diagnostic tests. And no genetic link has been firmly established.

If the feeling of fatigue persists over months, accompanied by symptoms such as dizziness, dry eyes, nausea, earaches, chest pains, bellyache, chronic cough or weight loss, doctors usually look into patient's medical history and undertake a detailed physical examination. They run a few standard tests to eliminate the presence of any specific ailment. In the absence of the same, they tend to treat CFS with mild medication, coupled with recommended behavioural changes. Patients are often advised not to overdose themselves with medicines; not to pop a pill for every ache and pain.

Now, the cause of chronic fatigue could be one or a combination of several factors listed below:

Hormonal problems

Sugar imbalance

The foods you eat

The environment, especially the air you breathe

Moulds, mites, allergies

Sleep and relaxation

Exercise

Depression

Dr. Ronald L. Hoffman in his book *Tired All the Time* (Poseidon Press) discusses these factors at length. But then he comes out with a few surprising findings about chronic fatigue—secrets that fly in the face of our conventional wisdom.

His first and most important finding: energy begets energy. There are people who attack their day with a gusto that seems to increase with each passing hour. They appear to be made of different stuff from the ordinary person. But they're not. People who put in tremendous energy are energized by their very activity. Physical activity oxygenates all parts of the body, including the brain. The result: more energy. According to Hoffman, once you've corrected any flaws in your lifestyle or diet or environment that may be contributing to your fatigue, then you'll find that energy begets energy.

His second finding: life is not a steady downhill process. While a certain decline in vitality is a natural consequence of ageing, your energy quotient can be sustained at high levels well through middle age and into your senior years.

His third finding; efforts to conserve energy can leave you more exhausted. Most people think resting a lot will cure their fatigue—yet it often makes it worse. Someone asking another to post a letter a few blocks away because of being too tired to walk up to the letterbox can be showing the fatigue that comes from too much rest. Hoffman has even discovered that when he was tired, sleep wasn't always the answer.

One more secret: stimulants may give you a short-term boost, but over the long run they can deplete you. Guzzling umpteen cups of coffee can keep you alert—but leave you ultimately depleted.

Another fact of fatigue; fatigue can sometimes be contagious—just like a yawn. When you sit long with someone who is depressed and fatigued, you may find yourself overcome by a draining ennui.

And Hoffman cautions people who actually use sugar as medicine for the feeling of fatigue or depression. Sugar does indeed change the brain chemistry, and could impart a sense of momentary wellbeing. But then sugar becomes a form of—somewhat akin to alcoholism.

Hoffman advises a switch over to a diet of protein and carbohydrates, which provide the body with slowly released and steady levels of sugar, thus reducing reliance on items rich in sugar.

Here is a guide to sugar content of some common foods (grams of sugar per 100 grams of food). While raisins and dates reach 64, bananas, apricots, grapes and apples range between 16 to 12, and oranges 9. Vegetables mostly stay below 9, with onions at 5 and cabbage at 2. Jams and chocolates touch 65, ice cream, 23, and Coca-Cola, 11.

And Hoffman advocates some simpler measures: drink more water, do breathing exercises, and sleep well.

Drinking Problems

Here are a few questions to test one's alcohol use. But these are worth answering only if you're going to be honest with yourself about your drinking.

Do you feel an urgency for the first drink?

Does a craving for the next follow it?

Do you tend to gulp down the first drink fairly fast—say, under ten minutes instead of the usual half an hour in social drinking"

Do you at times take an extra drink when someone is out of the room; you don't want that person to know how much you drink?

Do you tend to time your drinking so that others are not really aware of how much you're drinking?

Have you often had a drink last thing at night to help you get to sleep?

At a time when you'd anticipated having a drink, would you have one, even though the only drink available was the variety you don't normally fancy?

Do you suffer a preoccupation with where the next drink is going to come, and how you're going to get it?

Would you have a drink before you go out to a function that might be dry?

Would you find it strange to leave a good part of your drink?

Have you ever failed to prove to yourself the ability (a) not to drink before a certain time of the day, and (b) to give up alcohol for a week or a month or more?

Has anyone else (and that includes your spouse) expressed repeated serious concern about your drinking?

Are you aware from your experience that you commonly drink significantly more than you intend?

Do you sometimes berate yourself up about your drinking by calling yourself "weak-willed"?

Are you worried about your drinking?

A lot of "yes" answers imply that you may be developing a drink problem—a craving for alcohol for emotional comfort, not its social aspect. Your total intake of alcohol doesn't have to be heavy, but you have graduated from social drinking to habitual drinking.

Habitual drinkers are known to harbour some common notions about alcohol use. Yet on closer scrutiny, these come out more as magical myths.

"Life would be dull without a drink. In fact one can't laugh much without drinks."

"I won't know how to spend my evenings."

"Alcohol relaxes me, gives me confidence."

"I usually don't start drinking before sunset. Anyway only alcoholics drink in the morning."

"I only drink beer, no hard drinks (what about the quantity—alcohol is alcohol?)"

"I drink red wine which is said to be good for the heart (two large glasses make four measures)."

"I won't have a social life without alcohol."

"I'll never meet new people at parties if I stop drinking. In fact I can't go to parties if I stop drinking."

"People will find me boring if I don't drink."

"Everyone drinks these days, so I'll be the odd person out."

Women and Excessive Drinking

"There is nothing manly or heroic or glamorous about those who drink too much. In men it is crude and embarrassing; in women it is plain sickening."

— *A former British Secretary of State for Social Welfare*

Fifty years ago an Indian woman drinking at a party was a rarity. Nowadays, it's nothing unusual if a majority of women attending an upper-strata dinner accept alcohol.

Of course, most women don't make a beeline for the bar like their men: they stay in their seats looking for a little persuasion. And their acceptance of a drink is almost invariably accompanied by the phrase: "But a small one, please". To which a genial host responds by serving a standard measure. Indeed, quite a few women could be seen downing two to three stiff drinks before the customary late dinner without being any the worse for it.

Women show a marked preference for white drinks: gin, vodka, white rum. These are deemed milder than the brown ones (alcohol content is actually the same; in fact clearer drinks act quicker). Others rate white drinks as "cooling". Anyway, white drinks are less odiferous than the brown. Alcohol itself is odourless. The odour in drinks, commonly known as the 'drinker's breath', comes from congeners present in a drink. And the congener content is higher in long-maturing spirits such as whisky or brandy.

Our middle-class aversion to alcohol is fast whittling away. And with it a growing acceptance of women's social drinking. On occasions it's even encouraged as fashionable. And such social occasions can be quite frequent in some quarters.

Social drinking, seemingly harmless, poses its own perils. If Western experience is any guide, a minimum of 10 per cent of casual, social drinkers develop addictive, excessive drinking. Our middle-class drinking scene has yet to be surveyed in sufficient depth. One particular problem encountered in these surveys: middle-class drinkers tend to underreport their intake. Women are even more secretive about their drinking than men.

What constitutes excessive drinking? The current medical consensus sets the sensible limit at 14 units of alcohol per week for women and 21 units for men (the average woman has a smaller build than the average man, and women have a lower percentage of muscle than men to absorb alcohol). And no more than a couple of units per week for pregnant and lactating women, or even for those wanting to be pregnant. An added factor is the vulnerability of the menstrual cycle to alcohol.

Worldwide women of all ages drink less than men, and so encounter fewer alcohol-related problems. But then much of the discourse about female drinking implies a double standard. "Drinking, more so excessive drinking, is deemed morally inappropriate for women, let alone being more physically damaging," said Margaret Thatcher, the erstwhile British Prime Minister.

Amongst women, heavier drinking is getting associated with socio-economic status. Some poor ones may occasionally go on a drinking binge. But heavy drinking on a regular basis is mostly limited to upper-strata women. There is now considerable evidence that women who work, more so career women, are likely to be heavier drinkers than those who don't work—drink marking a break from work and used as a restorative, the way it is with men. Working women also have more opportunities of meeting men in drinking situations. Another likely group of heavier drinkers is of housewives, in whose well-to-do homes alcohol is routinely stocked and served. At a societal level ease of access and increased intake are linked.

Heavy drinking seems more common in younger women (below 45) than in older ones (over 60). Women who are separated, divorced or widowed appear to be more vulnerable. Again women with dependent children are apt to drink less than those without children.

Quite a few heavy women drinkers are known to believe that alcohol can lift their depression. While alcohol has sedative properties, whether it really helps to lift depression or not is debatable. Working women, worried about their shyness in company or nervousness in decision-making, may well be using alcohol to increase self-confidence.

Others are known to link their heavy drinking to a significant "life event"—bereavement, infertility, divorce, husband's infidelity, etc. Some psychologists, however, feel that heavy female drinking being highly stigmatized, these women may be trying to reduce their sense of stigma by ascribing their drinking problem to a specific precipitating event.

While women are generally more inclined than men to seek expert help for their health problems, they are less likely to seek similar help for a drinking problem, because of the greater stigma. Admission of heavy drinking often risks a disruption in marital relations. Some fear losing their children; social welfare agencies in several countries send small children of known heavy drinkers into custodial care. An excessive drinker may even find it difficult to raise the subject of alcohol consumption with her doctor, something that comes quite easy for men. This could well result in the doctor missing the connection between drink and a health affliction, even making a misdiagnosis. Or she may consider that her drink problem is too trivial to take up with the doctor.

Health educationalists had assumed that an emphasis on "safe" levels of consumption would restrict heavy drinking. At least the middle-classes, with their heightened health consciousness, would follow the "official" advice. Evidence shows that people do not see drinking as a major health concern. The public remains confused about what levels of intake are really harmful and the relative strength of different drinks.

Indoor Pollutants

Our exposure to most toxic pollutants could be several times higher in indoor environments than it is outdoors. However, whereas there is much public concern with city air pollution, precious little attention is focused on indoor pollutants.

Take a typical household with small children—a toddler mouthing anything that comes to hand, crawling under the dining table, or sucking its soiled fingers, and a bigger kid hugging the dog, playing with stuffed toys, or rolling on the carpet. It's small children who are most exposed to indoor pollutants, whether from dust mites in carpets or pesticides sticking to toys, or contaminants carried by pets. That way, kids are little guinea pigs testing the toxicity of whatever pollutants are in the home.

Children are more at risk than adults, because they have a higher metabolic rate and their organs are still developing. Weight for weight, they inhale much more than adults, while their lungs can be irritated by relatively lower levels of air pollution.

To a housewife, dust settling on sofas and beds, carpets and clothes is more of a nuisance than anything else—something to be dusted off regularly. Hardly a thought is given to the fact that house dust is host to millions of germs. And the most prolific of all are the dust mites.

If these bothersome creatures would only manifest themselves like flies or mosquitoes, a housewife could swat them or train a flit gun at them. But these eight-legged cousins to the spider and the tick are less than a half millimetre long, and mostly invisible. And then dust mites play safe by sneaking into carpets, bedclothes, stuffed furniture, and similar soft objects.

Dust mites, one of the 20,000 species of mites, are running no risk of extinction, though they die by the millions each day. Female dust mites which constitute half of the population make sure of this by laying over 50 eggs a day.

What do dust mites feed on? They are meat eaters, and curiously enough, their only diet consists of flakes of skin that humans constantly shed.

Each dust mite produces about 20 fecal pellets a day. And it is these waste particles that trigger allergies in people, even asthma. Infants are particularly vulnerable to dust mites.

Affluent homes with wall-to-wall carpeting, heavy curtains, and cushioned sofas prove an excellent habitat for these invisible devils.

Carpets are indeed the biggest source of toxic substances—the largest reservoirs of dust in the house. And they pose the highest health risks for infants and toddlers. There's plenty of opportunity for busy little hands to pick up various contaminants during the course of a day as they play on carpeted floors.

Besides dust mites, plenty of pesticides are found deep inside carpets—often deep among the fibres and the backing, and beyond the reach of vacuuming. Pesticides, whether sprayed in rooms or on the lawn, cling to shoes and pet's paws, and then get rubbed off onto carpeting. A typical sample of household carpet dust sent to a lab would disclose significant presence of heavy metals and toxic chemicals, such as lead, mercury, cadmium, pesticides and hydrocarbons. Leaving shoes at the doorstep is a good measure to minimize indoor pollutants.

Thick doormats do help. Better still, people should leave their shoes at the door. Weekly vacuuming of carpets becomes a must. And the necessity of more passes over the area of rugs near the entrance, and other areas that receive a lot of traffic. A vacuum cleaner with a power head is more effective as it picks up three to six times as much dust as one without power brushes. Anyway vacuuming is vastly superior to using dusters or brooms; the latter becomes more of an exercise in rearranging the dust.

For people with small kids or with adults allergic to dust mites, tiled floors with scattered rugs prove more environmental friendly than wall-to-wall carpeting. Luckily, as a people, we are given to washing our floors or wiping them daily with wet cloth. As to floor rugs, experts recommend deep-cleaning once a year by professional cleaners.

Dust mites are also found in abundance in beds, where they feed on the dead skin shed by sleepers. It's a good idea to cover all mattresses in airtight, washable plastic fabrics. Bed sheets should be washed weekly in very hot water to get rid of mites and their droppings. And better keep pets away from beds.

Dust filters in air-conditioners do remove much of airborne particles of dust. But then these filters have to be cleaned frequently.

People who use pesticides indoors may inadvertently expose small children to significant contamination, even if they're careful to keep kids and chemicals apart. Chemicals evaporate, drift from place to place, precipitate back onto carpets, toys and other soft household objects, with which children come in contact. And pesticides persist for months indoors because they are sheltered from sun, rain and other forces that quickly degrade them outdoors.

8

Married Life in Middle Years

Married Life in Middle Age

Much gets written and talked about the married life of younger people. However, the married life of older couples is still shrouded a good deal in secrecy and silence.

This was understandable when life expectancy was low half a century back. Now most of us expect to live into our sixties and seventies if not beyond. Heightened health awareness coupled with medical advances further enables us to stay in better physical shape during our middle years.

The departure of daughters and eventually of sons is experienced as a loss, more so by the mother. The departure removes a whole range of activities from her. Less food to be bought, fewer demands made on her cooking, less of laundry and cleaning. And then there's the constant reminder of the "empty nest".

This return to one-to-one relationship can in some cases herald an upsurge of marital nearness or tenderness. The couples come closer; they have more time for each other, and more privacy. They accept more attention for themselves.

On the other hand, serious differences which had lain smothered in the bringing-up phase of children, may now surface up. Some couples may discover to their distress they have little or nothing in common; the only common thing was children.

"In the absence of two disabilities—actual disease and the belief that 'the old' are or should be asexual—sexual requirements and sexual capacity are lifelong," says Dr. Alex Comfort. Human beings that way are unique in the constancy of their sexual activity, and unlike other animals, it's more re-creative than procreative. We human are easily 'turned-on' sexually. The female breast has become more an erotic symbol than an instrument of lactation. Figure-conscious women now manage to remain trim and attractive far into their middle years. Money and power work wonders on male masculinity. And the "madness of the middle age" is not a myth.

A couple's sexual life, however, begins to diverge as time passes. The husband's sexual drive diminishes (a biological phenomenon related to age) whilst the wife's remains unchanged or may even increase (there's no such direct link with age). Again, there is no evidence that menopause interferes with sexual interest and activity.

There seems to be a definite connection between good, continuing sex and the basic components of a good marriage relationship. Sexual intercourse in middle age—besides being mutually pleasurable to the couple—reinforces a women's sexual identity as a woman, as separate from being a mother or daughter.

A few words for the wife.

Your middle-aged mate usually needs some tactful handling; he can get so easily put off sex. Take care that a particular evening or afternoon (many older men stay more active at midday) proceeds without a jarring note. Don't shrug him off watching your favoured TV serial or in the midst of darning. Be a bit cuddly instead of always brisk and efficient or busy with house chores.

Researchers have consistently reported upon a facet of married life in middle age; that over time, women become more assertive, and men more yielding. Women became more sure of their opinions, men less dogmatic. Not that they lose their old traits but new ones get added; older men and women acquiring supplementary qualities that are conventionally defined as appropriate to the opposite sex. Whereas young women are tender to infants, now grandfathers become unbelievably soft to small children. Old men engage in touching for touching sake—not as a wayside station to sex—the kind of thing that is associated with women. Some husbands have trouble coming to terms with this growing assertiveness of their mates as if their leadership in the house is getting challenged.

The middle-age marriage scenario could well be visualized as falling under three broad patterns. No doubt, numerous variations are there in-between.

One group is of couples who are constantly fighting with each other, with each fight a temporary victory or defeat. Such partners would be lost without this constant sparring. The arguments are always supposedly about an issue but in reality it's more a question of showing who's temporarily in charge. Fighting for them is in fact a means by which they reach out to each other. One imagines, things could be a little better if he kept a good deal to his study room or was occupied in some other pursuit instead of meddling with the affairs of the kitchen or otherwise encroaching upon her turf.

Another category of couples is those who grow indifferent to each other; the keyword to their life is boredom. They eat, sleep and go out together in a mechanical manner. The other's presence is mainly a means of avoiding acute loneliness. The two are bored with each other but rarely quarrel. Expecting little from the other, their chief consolation is the unchangeable routine of their lives. It is said that such a situation can be partially eased if the couple keep a dog, or better still a dog each.

The third group would be couples who take considerable interest in each other's feelings, emotions and activities. They regard their spouse as far more than the man or woman they eat and sleep with. They tender to do things together and achieve a togetherness which is constantly changing and growing. Marriage inequalities—marriage is not exactly an equal institution—get ironed out over years of such living.

Possibly they do things for each other without a daily balancing of accounts; the obligations seem to have been earned over a lifetime of caring and love. Each other's defects are underplayed. "If his wife had any fault, he had grown so used to them that he failed to notice them," reminisced Benjamin Franklin.

Mulling Over the Middle Years

What turn out to be our happier years, the middle years of 45 to 65, or the younger ones of 25 to 45? To many the question may sound ridiculous; why, surely the younger years. The question assumes added importance as most of us—courtesy medical science—are now set to reach our middle years.

Admittedly, the answer in each case will be a highly personal one; how we happen to assess our middle years or picture what these would be. Yet in this context, the four sequential novels of John Updike—*Rabbit Run, Rabbit Redux, Rabbit Is Rich, and Rabbit at Rest*—make interesting reading. Their common hero, Harry "Rabbit" Angstrom, is 26, 36, 46 and 56, respectively, in these four books.

There is the traditional view that the middle years are a period of decline, on a spectrum from fatigue through multiplied losses to despair. Head hair recedes or turns grey while you have hair coming out of nose and ears. Possibly a paunch that refuses to go away. For putting on socks or even trousers, it feels safer to sit down. A noon nap becomes a must, and teeth decay. Filings come out or there is loss of teeth. Anyway every meal involves some breaking of enamel and a great deal of tooth-picking. It now takes more time to recall names or remember what we did the day before. Ageing is so emphatically assumed as a no-win process.

Until recently, the decline version of the midlife story has prevailed. We have been masochistically eager to accept bad news about our idle age and ageing. Enormous numbers of no-longer young have personally let themselves become melancholy comparers, looking fondly but myopically back, feeling somehow sure that life is a diminished thing. And literature representing this state of mind has often been called 'realistic', as if only a pessimistic view of life could be called real.

John Updike and a few other modern novelists like Saul Bellow are coming out with a different version in the last two decades. The progress narrative of the middle years of their heroes and heroines is not all inevitably downhill. These writers attribute psychic resilience to their midlife characters, and often endow them with sensitivity or composure or autonomy. Instead of a purely decline plot, they want their readers to consider the possibility that life can be constructed as a process of losing false fears or our overly pessimistic anticipations. A new genre is emerging in which there are heroes and heroines in their middle years; new plots of r-covery and development in those years; and favourable views of midlife outlooks, of midlife parenting and midlife subjectivity. They are not "heroes" and "heroines" in the classical mould, but they have resistances, strengths and ingenious mental feints.

The authors proceed on the premise that our character is not all fixed early in life as was the persistent older myth. They go along with the new consensus in serious psychodynamic theory that development is probably a life-long process. And here, self-esteem strengthens the development of character, with the power to imagine a better future self and the striving to become it.

To write midlife fiction, however, the author had better experience midlife himself. John Updike, born in 1932, was going through nearly the same age as his hero Rabbit when he wrote about him. As he has aged, his hero has aged also—one can discern an autobiographical element in these novels. And another thing: to understand midlife fiction or at least to care enough to read it at all, readers must overcome a certain mental block. Readers have to get over their past study of literature where a middle-aged person is often a figure of fun when in love or when otherwise hogging significant attention.

Of course, the protagonists in the new midlife novels don't get everything they want; some losses are inevitable, whether in the death of the dear ones or the problems with health and vitality. Yet the balance precariously held at times, often tips in favour of the middle-aged. The job troubles and the money troubles could loom less and the marriage relationship is usually happier—at least more understanding and less tumultuous.

In John Updike's third book, Rabbit is rich at 46. The earlier life of financial struggles and worries is happily past. And in the fourth book, Rabbit at 56, starts having greater respect for the views of his wife, who is fast acquiring a businesswoman's efficiency in her middle age.

In the middle years, sexuality recedes relative to other interests. The sexual perspective undergoes an unimagined change; an excellent meal may become nearly as inviting, and so also a good night of rest. Instead of the wife's being frequently cajoled into sex, she is now alert to every signal. Sizeable periods of celibacy in the marital bed no longer feel like a deprivation. And then there are the familiar things like occasional impotence or selfish orgasm, and increasing pornographic fantasies of other women.

"Midlife is a contrast-gainer," says Bellow, then in his sixties. To feel good about the middle years it is helpful to have had a miserable young adulthood. This is not such a difficult requirement, considering that most youthful years are often scenes of struggle, tension and worry, even of adjustment problems in marriage. Bringing up small children is another area of anxiety or even guilt. Working women with little children to bring up have a particularly harrying time. Why more of us don't prize our middle years is a mystery. Presumably one thing that stops us from doing so is the phenomenon whereby we tend to prettify our past.

Death is nearer in middle age but the dread of death is usually less than what is commonly assumed. One readily acknowledges the inevitability of death and accepts it more serenely than in younger years. Middle age, that way, is part of the process of completion of a life, and the more one completes, the more one loses fear of death.

Some of this emerging literature is taking a kinder view of middle age than it was there before. Apparently this looks more in line with the reality of middle-class middle age today. And the expectations for tomorrow are even better.

Staying Incompatible for Fifty Years

If compatibility were a necessary condition of happy marriage, then ours would rate as a serious mistake made fifty years ago. Theoretically, marriage is all about two persons becoming one. But that sort of fusion has made precious little headway in ours.

As I try to figure out areas of compatibility, I actually end up with a long list of incompatibilities. How the marriage survives—in fact, it fares surprisingly well—is somewhat of a mystery.

I am an early riser, often at the computer by 5 a.m. She never wakes before 7; says her best sleep happens between 5 and 7. That means I've to sneak out of bed without putting on a light, hoping not to hit my shins against a piece of furniture. She's a night person, often reads a book or watches television till midnight. Perforce, I burrow my face under the bedclothes or don an eye-shade. Luckily, the moment I hit the bed, I'm often asleep.

I eat fast, heap everything on one plate, and gorge myself without making much distinction between various items. She eats slow, and is picky with what she eats. Often I finish the main course when she's half through, and then I wait impatiently for the dessert, drumming the table with my fingers. Piqued, at times she lets me have the sweet straightway, while her own she carries to the family room.

Even television we watch differently. I prefer to watch attentively in relative silence. She can easily combine it with ironing, telephoning, and conversation. And while I'd like to slide into a comfortable seat, she prefers to perch on a sofa stool; easier to get up frequently for various household chores. My main watching is sports—cricket, football, golf—she favours romantic serials and tear-jerkers. At times, I have to move to the living-room TV set for a prolonged sports viewing, as she takes over the main one.

She loves parties, birthdays, and fun-shopping. I have a hearty distaste of shopping. Having known prices prevalent in the 1930–40s, to me everything appears atrociously over-priced.

And birthdays don't excite me, anyway not my own.

The list of incompatibilities goes on endlessly. Yet I can't imagine being married to anyone else. We're together, but it's not because of compatibility. Each one of us thinks the other is adorable; at least that's the way I think.

Retirement, a Second Marriage

What happens to a marriage when a husband and wife find themselves together 24 hours a day, maybe for the first time in their lives?

Prior to his retirement the man went out to work. The evening might be spent discussing the day's events and other people's problems; the couple's own getting side-stepped. Unfilled parts of a marriage can be masked by being busy.

But what happens when the work life ceases? The supportive job routine is gone. The network of colleagues virtually cut off. The only outlet left is often the marriage partner; grown-up children may have also departed by this time.

Retirement has been described as a second marriage. And it can be quite a difficult marriage to start with — till the parties adjust themselves anew to the enforced togetherness.

A retirement is seen to be accompanied by four fearful demons: isolation, boredom, reduced income (plus poorer housing, loss of help and facilities), and fall in self-esteem. All the more damaging to one's self-esteem if retired at the relatively early age of mandatory retirement (58 or 55), with the physical and mental faculties intact. No wonder, people are at such pains to prolong their employment or clutch at any alternative avenue of work. It's here that the self-employed like lawyers and doctors are the subject of most envy.

Let's face it, we live in a society where our work defines us; well-nigh justifies us. In such a scenario, retirement can be tantamount to a near total loss of identity, another word for defeat. Unless, through some spirited activity, one can achieve the more acceptable status termed "keeping busy".

What about the one, who frankly admits, "I'm doing nothing", or quips, "I'm killing time till time comes to kill me."

Hearing a sorry response like this, his questioners look puzzled for an instant, then are startled as the words sink in; finally they stare at him in silent embarrassment. Plainly, he is withering away before their very eyes. Admiration these days is reserved for elders who successfully challenge their biological clocks with prodigious feats of energy and accomplishments.

After retirement, home becomes the central focus. A retiree is apt to cling to its resources. But here again he may discover to his dismay that the two of them—he and his wife—are one too many in the house, more so if it's a small house.

However circumspect he may be, he still prowls on his mate's turf. And interlopers arouse hostility. How would he have reacted if his wife had hung around his office all day? Similarly, she may feel herself maddeningly in a bind like a Siamese twin. No privacy for little things. If she's sorting out her clothes, he comments. When she talks on the telephone, he's listening or even butting in. Any minor household mishap, such as china plate breaking, gets known to him immediately.

Housewives commonly complain of overwork with a husband at home when it should be the other way about. Here's a handyman, available all the time to fix up things, tend to the garden patch and answer the doorbell. The last chore he possibly welcomes. Callers bring some excitement to life even if it is an unwanted salesman or a suspicious mendicant.

But there is something worse for her than sharing the same turf. A sense of sadness floats in the air. She comes to hate her husband's retirement because it makes her feel old. You are diminished in an unexpected way, being married to a pensioner.

There is a plethora of guidebooks for the retiree, with statistics giving him dire warnings of death rates jumping markedly in the third and fourth years after retirement.

If you can't live comfortably on your pension, plus rent if any, better pocket your pride and take to paid work. Nothing is worse for marital harmony than the combination of enforced togetherness and the paucity of purse.

Things look a bit brighter if your wife still has her job—presumably younger to you by several years. But then you have to lay the welcome mat on her return (and no cribbing if she's late). Run a comb through what's left of your hair. Usher her in, give her the best seat. And don't pester her forthwith as to what transpired at the office. She will talk of these things in her own good time. What she hates is to be routinely interrogated on return.

Your own distress stories—the sweeper not turning up for the day or the bananas going bad—can wait till she has time to settle down. And, by the way, when you are alone at home, don't wander too much in the neighbourhood—keep the shame of your unemployment to yourself.

When both the partners are grounded home, a fine balance has to be struck between togetherness and aloneness. Regular spells of reading in a separate room—you can call it your study—are a help; nobody minds even if you doze off there. But lolling away in bed or on the living room sofa with a magazine or paper is another matter.

And it may not be a bad idea to be shaved and dressed up before breakfast time; this brings back some semblance of your former work-life. Continuing clad in crumpled pyjamas and dragging a newspaper through half the day is a sorry sight.

Time-consuming games like golf and bridge can get you out of her hair. And, if both share these hobbies, you can play golf in separate foursomes and bridge on different club tables.

All this doesn't mean 'the second marriage' of retirement is devoid of fun. But it calls for care and consideration, perhaps far in excess of what you brought to 'the first'.

Sex in Middle Years

According to one recent survey in the UK, youth finishes at 32 while middle age starts by 54. Take a few myths about sex and ageing:

Most older men lose their ability and desire to have sex.

Coital satisfaction decreases considerably after menopause.

Older women who still enjoy sex were probably nymphomaniacs when they were younger.

Sexual desire and the sexual ability of the old (conveniently classified as men and women over 60 or even over 65) has been the subject of much public misconceptions and conflicting opinions. There is the image of the aged male as an asexual, impotent being. Others assume sexual perversions as common in old age, especially indecent familiarity with children. While some decline in sexual interest and activity does accompany the ageing process, current studies seem to indicate that a person's sex drive remains fairly constant well into advanced age.

The pioneering Kinsey studies on women (1953) reported little evidence of any ageing in the sexual capacities of women. Masters and Johnson (1966) concluded that "there is no time limit drawn by the advancing years to female sexuality". Elderly persons in reasonably good health are known to have continued sexually active into their seventies, eighties, and even nineties. Pfeiffer's survey in 1972 of 62 men and women between the ages of 66–71 (of Americans selected at random) showed that 48% were having intercourse once a month, and 28% once a week or more. Only 24% had given it up. This also indicated a dramatic shift in attitudes from procreative sex to re-creative sex. We may not be doing as well in health, living standards and attitudes, yet human beings everywhere are nearly the same.

The decline in sexual activity in older people is ascribed not so much to a decline in desire; there may be other inhibiting factors like the lack of a partner, physical disability, negative societal attitudes or psychological scars of retirement and powerlessness. For instance, sex may cease for an older woman with the death of her husband (widowed old men seem sexually more active than elderly widows), or her husband's inability to perform or his loss of interest in sex with her. Here, women labour under a double disadvantage; they are generally married to men older than they. So they cease having intercourse approximately six years before men. A large majority of older women attribute responsibility for cessation of intercourse to their partners, and older males often own the same. Of course, there are women "who never have been too happy about sex during most of their lives and find in menopause or in their advancing years a respectable reason for ending a duty that has always been onerous or distasteful to them".

Studies and surveys on human sexuality have proliferated in the last fifty years. Sexual research is no longer considered "so mysterious and spiritual". And even older people—long neglected in this field—are receiving increasing attention. The book *Human Sexual Response* of Masters and Johnson devotes nearly 50 pages to it. With life expectancy going up there will be a lot more people living beyond 65—and healthier, too, with improving health standards

Ageing brings certain physical changes. Overall, the age-related changes in the male reproduction system include (1) decrease in the size and firmness of testes, (2) decline in seminal production though sperm formation continues into eighties, (3) slow development of excitement and erection, and (4) lengthened refractory (recovery) period. The stage immediately preceding orgasm in younger men—the anticipatory feeling of orgasmic inevitability—is mostly missing. Again, the contractions of the rectal sphincter, which in younger men occur regularly during the orgasmic experience, decrease in frequency with ageing. A smaller quantity of fluid is ejected with less force. While the refractory period in young men may be a matter of minutes, a man of sixty five may take about 12 to 24 hours to have another orgasm. Again de-tumescence immediately after ejaculation is relatively rapid in an ageing male.

In females, besides sterility, ageing brings in shrinkage of the external genitalia and a decrease in pubic hair. Uterus shortens in size, too. The physiological counterpart of the male erection is vaginal lubrication. While young women experience vaginal lubrication within 10 to 30 seconds, women in their sixties take from one to three minutes. There is also much less of it. All this can cause irritation especially as the vaginal walls become thinner. A good deal of the difficulty can, however, be remedied through use of an artificial lubricant.

Some of the health disorders that interfere with sexual activity in old age are alcoholism, heavy smoking, stroke, arthritis, diabetes, cardiac weaknesses and prostate problems. Obesity and excessive consumption of food also have a tendency to repress sexual feelings.

The dangers of sexual intercourse to the damaged heart have been long exaggerated. The average heart rate during coitus is 120 beats per minute which is about the same level reached in light jogging. The oxygen supply used in sexual activity is similar to that required for a brisk walk. Death from a heart attack during coitus is highly unlikely. Men after heart attacks are usually allowed by their doctors to engage in sexual intercourse under carefully regulated conditions.

Other sexual dysfunctions like secondary impotence, premature ejaculation (less than a minute after intromission) or retarded ejaculation (extreme prolongation) are not the exclusive province of the elderly; the young can suffer from the same, too. The good news is that in a majority of such cases competent counseling and treatment (as distinguished from quackery) succeeds.

A failure in bed, once or twice at crucial moments, can set in motion an unfortunate train of events. The husband may altogether withdraw from lovemaking fearing failure—the fear of failure itself is paralyzing. Men are rather too proud or reticent in these matters and just prefer to throw in the towel. She may misinterpret it all as being no longer attractive to him, or "too old for that sort of thing".

Leaving aside the physical problems accompanying age, societal factors also inhibit sexual activity in older people. If society insists that sex is inappropriate for the aged, the people themselves internalize this belief and give it up. The phenomenon is known as 'sociogenic ageing', imaginary or imposed ageing with little physical basis. Grandmothers, for instance, are supposed to have banished all thoughts of sex. Older couples are routinely denied the privacy extended to the young. The love life of old people attracts many a joke and mockery, or even resentment with some young of the family.

These negative social attitudes towards physical love among older people in various cultures and societies (ours as negative as any) will operate as a serious deterrent till such times as they undergo a change.

Ageing Losses and Morale

"To be seventy years young is sometimes more cheerful and hopeful than to be forty years old," says a wit.

Recent research reveals that older persons suffering diminishments—losses in health, reduced income, constricted social relationships, widowhood, and occupational retirement—often report surprisingly high levels of life satisfaction. What could be the explanation for the seeming paradox?

Old age is admittedly an embarrassment, despite all the encouraging things said about ageing. Old people, however healthy and substantial, are somewhat disconcerting, as they signify the nearness of death.

Entry into old age brings major changes in role and status. And these are mostly in the shape of losses.

A prime factor is job retirement, with its loss of occupational activity and status. And while science has been successful in prolonging the average life-span, society continues to retire compulsorily a lot of people at a prescribed age, irrespective of their being healthy and useful. Sixty, it's quipped, is the age when one acquires sufficient experience to lose one's job.

People who retired are more likely to feel old than their age—vis-à-vis peers who are still working. This causes retirees (mostly male retirees) to experience a reduction in feelings of confidence and personal worth. Some try to assuage the situation by maintaining identification with their former occupational status: "retired doctor," "retired professor," "retired colonel," and so on. That way, the highly educated experience the least perceived status loss after retirement, whereas persons in low-status occupations lose most in self-esteem. The latter's position is apt to suffer a significant drop even in the eyes of their wives.

Older individuals commonly find that occupational retirement is followed by diminished income, lessened physical mobility, a decline in health and vitality, and a constriction of the social world through the death of a spouse and close friends. Each of these changes has a distressing effect upon the individual's psychological adaptation; their occurrence in rapid succession makes them an even greater threat to the retention of good morale and mental stability in old age.

The above view of ageing as a detrimental process suggests that older persons should show considerable demoralization as life changes progressively attenuate their standing in society. Previous research had often demonstrated that morale diminishes with losses in health and shrunken social life. In the realm of health and vigour, ageing not only means dangerous diseases but may bring one disability after another: impaired sight, troublesome teeth, poor hearing (an underestimated disability when it becomes a problem in conversation), and waning of smell sense (an underrated disability). More and more doctors start figuring in one's telephone book and less and less of friends.

Of late, however, several investigators are finding that aged persons with deprived status often report surprisingly high levels of life satisfaction. Older persons, it appears, "come to terms" with their deprivations. According to Edward Diener, an American psychologist noted for his researches on happiness, "the old as a group have more life satisfaction than the young. The minds of the young are full of the things they want to achieve and have not, whereas most of the elderly have either achieved what they wanted or made their peace with the fact that they never will."

Several explanations have been offered for the retention of relatively high morale in later life. One is the disengagement theory; an older person's withdrawal from society. Individuals are observed replacing many established values with a desire for an isolated, static, self-centred existence. This reorientation results in new contentment, despite the onset of an objectively deprived life.

The more plausible explanation is the reference-group theory, whereby a point of reference is provided with which an older person can compare his or her life situations.

An important aspect of this comparative function is that many negative stereotypes are applied to the "aged" as a social category in today's society. Old age is seen by young and old both as a time of diminished physical activity, absentmindedness, social isolation, poor health, increased dependency, sexual abstinence, and the like. Comparisons by older persons of their personal situations with those of the other "aged" are likely to be cast against these negative stereotypes.

In that sense, the stereotypes have a positive function; they reassure persons who are undergoing age-related losses that their experiences are neither uncommon nor as severe as experienced by most aged persons. The individual's comparison of his own situation with that of the stereotyped "aged" reference group may thus serve as a buffer against demoralization that would otherwise be expected to accompany the losses of role and status incurred with ageing.

Older People Tripping and Falling

Older people are known to hurt themselves more than younger ones when they trip and fall. Indeed, such falls are responsible for the majority of injuries suffered by people over 65.

The phenomenon has been the subject of much research in recent times.

Mark Grabiner of the Cleveland Clinic in the United States has conducted elaborate laboratory experiments on old and young in tripping and falling. He found that the young trip as regularly as the old, and their upper body pitches as forward when they trip as of the old. He had expected older people with weaker muscles to pitch further forward. To his surprise, it was observed that strong or weak, young or old, people tilted at the same angle when tripping.

The young, however, almost always managed to stay on their feet. When one foot was tripped, they immediately put forward the other leg as if hopping, pushing it higher in the air than in a normal step. This won them some extra time to recover. Older people weren't often able to push off the other leg that fast and forcefully.

Of course, older people with a slow shuffling gait bought a little extra time to react when tripped; their older counterparts walking briskly with confidence came down quicker.

According to James Ashton-Miller at the University of Michigan, these studies point to one crucial factor; the importance of muscle power, particularly in the calf. By power he means not merely the force a muscle can exert but also how fast it can produce that force. Older people not only have twice the reaction time of younger ones, their muscles take twice as long to reach their maximum force.

The good news is that at any age muscle is trainable. Exercises like skipping, dancing or fast walking can increase the power of the calf muscles. And this can significantly reduce injuries suffered by older people in falls when tripping.

Older women, often leading sedentary lives, are especially advised to strengthen their calf muscles through suitable exercise. Because of their weaker bones, they tend to incur more serious injuries when they fall.

Affluent Oldsters

The Khosla couple, Rajiv, 72, and Radha, 67, are today's affluent oldsters. With property values having risen fast in Delhi, they now enjoy a high rental income, coupled with steady returns from a few sound investments. And the two of them live in a commodious house of their own.

The Khoslas' two children are well-settled; the son in New York and the married daughter in Bombay. And the couple stays unburdened by any financial commitments or loans.

The Khoslas manage an enviable lifestyle: a chauffeur, a live-in cook, a maid, a night watchman, and a part-time gardener. They play golf thrice a week at Delhi Golf Club and bridge thrice at the Gymkhana Club. They lead a fairly busy social life, with its complement of dinners and parties.

They have two longish holidays in a year—one to the USA and the other to an Indian hill station. With no life-threatening health problems, the couple is looking forward to another ten years of active existence together, and that includes a big bash on their 50th marriage anniversary falling due in four years.

What they wish most dearly is independent ageing; staying together in their own home, with no devastating physical disabilities—they fear death much less than disability. Both of them dread the prospect of being physically dependent on their children or any others; they only want to rely on servants or paid para-medical attendants.

Money-wise, the Khoslas seem to be far more comfortable than their children, who are still struggling with all the demands of children's education, expensive housing, and the manifold requirements of present day consumerism. Indeed, the oldsters keep on giving costly gifts to their children and grandchildren—yearning for nothing in return except love or at least respect. Possibly they have spent more money on their grandchildren's toys than the parents. And much of the jewellery, silk carpets, and cut-glass curios in their children's homes have been gifted by them.

The Khoslas are not an isolated phenomenon; their numbers may well be running into lakhs. And in the next thirty years these could run into millions. The process is sure to accelerate with the spread of affluence. Many of those who have made money in the era of economic liberalization will be tomorrow's oldsters. And people would not only be living longer, many would remain fairly active in their older years.

One thing markedly distinguishes today's affluent oldsters from the moneyed oldies of pre-inflation era, and that is the attitude towards the spending of money. To the traditional oldies, the ruling prices are rather shocking. That makes them very unwilling to spend money on consumer goods or services. What to say of spending money on others, they are loath to spend it on themselves. Anyway, they were attuned to see frugality as virtue, squandering as sin.

Today's affluent oldsters are mentally adjusted to the modern phenomenon of rising prices. And they stand strongly touched by the current world-wide consumerist culture. Blessed with spare cash, they are spending as never before, spending more aggressively than any older consumer group before them.

In this context, better housing assumes importance. Old-style bathrooms and kitchens, deemed obsolete, are being modernized fast. Even if the oldsters are hesitant, their adult children often living with them are forcing the pace. And so also additions and renovations to homes in the shape of extra rooms, enclosing verandahs, replacing old flooring, changing lights, installing cooling systems, and a host of other improvements deemed necessary these days.

Affluent oldsters are heavy consumers of health services: specialist consultation for ears, eyes, teeth, bones, heart, blood pressure, and men's urology problems. With almost everybody over sixty wearing glasses of some sort, the demand is for quality spectacles. Expensive capping of decayed teeth and the state-of-art hearing aids are common, along with women visiting beauty parlours and fighting their wars against wrinkles.

Today's affluent oldsters are displaying a pronounced down-ageing trend. Sixty-five is taken as the beginning of the second half of life, not the beginning of the end. Among them, the word "elderly" is meant more for someone over 79. There's the heightened quest for longer life and, more so, healthier life. People are getting increasingly particular about the food they eat, the water they drink, and the air they breathe. They exercise, and continue with sex into middle age.

The cutting edge of the down-ageing trend today is not so much the age aspect; it's the older people in search of a good time. They are shedding off some of the traditional reserve and stiffness of age and are taking more to fun activities of the young. And they seem to enjoy the relief these bring them from the cares of a mature age. Visiting funfairs, playing children's games, picnicking like youngsters, eating ice cream cones at wayside stalls, and dressing as youngsters are part of this change. Author John Javna has even come out with a book on elder fun, *Cool Tricks! A Grown-Up's Guide to All the Neat Things You Never Learned to Do as a Kid.*

These oldsters have the time to travel and the money. They prefer package tours. That saves them the botheration of undertaking detailed travel arrangements, and it's safer, health-wise, in the company of acquaintances. Of late, luxury cruises are gaining in popularity. There is the feel of a "soft" adventure, coupled with assured boarding and lodging, and a gratifying freedom from hassles of traveling to new places.

This approach towards feeling better and having more fun in one's ripe age has important implications for the market, especially when the numbers involved are escalating and their buying power growing considerable. The market has to cater to their needs, without reminding them that they are getting old.

9

What Makes a Marriage!

Secret of a Good Marriage

Joan Erikson, the wife of the famous psychoanalyst Erik Erikson and a scholar in her own right, was once asked what could be the secret of their celebrated marriage. Eriksons had been happily married for sixty years and were known for radiating mutual love and respect in each other's company.

"Well, that's easy," she said without hesitation. "A sense of humour. Humour is what keeps everything in balance."

Over and over again, it has been observed that shared laughter happens to be an important bond between happy couples. Not laughter in the sense of jokes making the rounds but something deeper. It's a state of marriage where the partners continue to find each other interesting, almost 'funny'.

Happily married couples have an intimate way of relating to each other. And this connection they are often seen to be keeping through a mild sort of spontaneous bantering. A majority of happily married couples are to a degree playful. A light-hearted attitude towards each other keeps them from acting defensive, combative or argumentative.

The same factor, it seems, was operating between my parents. They enjoyed an enviably happy marriage extending over sixty-five years. As children we would hear father's marital banter, sometimes we also joining in the fun. If mother got upset misplacing her bunch of keys, he would banter about the manner in which she kept the bunch, while helping in the search. Father also had a knack of relating petty office incidents in their comic context. In later years when mother gained in self-confidence and education, she bantered in her own inimitable style. And she learnt to laugh over little household mishaps.

Humour, even otherwise, has its uses. Few strategies are more useful in defusing frustration or tension or restoring a wounded ego. No tool is better than humour for handling petty irritations that often cause disproportionate hurt and anger.

Here are a few allied do's and don'ts for a happy marriage.

Learn to laugh at yourself.

Stay away from ultimatums.

Learn to deflect occasional uncalled-for comments.

Accept apologies gracefully.

Allow your partner a few eccentricities.

Stay away from comparisons.

And don't let your children come between you.

When Silence is Gold

In marital matters, if speech is silver, silence is sometimes gold.

Communication is the buzz word these days. Most of the current problems—political and social, marital and sexual—are said to be a consequence of poor communication between the parties. To its votaries, every situation was capable of being resolved with better communication.

Married couples are encouraged to ventilate their mutual grievances, to speak these out instead of bottling them up. Marriage counsellors extol the rewards of communication, and marriage manuals sing the virtues of it. Wives are particularly advised to break through the centuries of silence that women had imposed on themselves, more so when nature had endowed them with better verbalizing ability than men.

Generally, our impulse is to react the moment something goes wrong. But why approach the problem the way a child does? Rather than bursting forth right away, you could think over the problem. Similarly if you are required to react to an idea, you can delay your response and thus give yourself some perspective on the issue.

In work places when someone comes up with an idea, the good executive responds, "That's interesting. Let me think about it." But when one's spouse brings out anything new, it could often evoke an instant retort, "You know I don't like that." Why not say, "Let me think about it and I'll get back to you." Allowing some time between introduction and discussion of a new idea, or an old gripe, gives you time to weigh how you really feel about it without the pressure of having to give an instant response.

When you discover that your spouse is in an ugly or unreasonable mood, that's not the time to talk about your complaints or pursue any controversial suggestions. Persons in such mood are apt to say things that should remain unsaid. And there are some things that should never be said between spouses. For example, it's wise never to comment unfavourably on your mate's family—mother, father, sister, whoever. He can himself say he is like his father, but his wife should not say that even semi-affectionately. It can cause trouble, and it leaves her open to accusation of being just like her mother.

Wives are advised to resist the urge to use post-great-sex euphoria as an opportunity to discuss ticklish things like their money problems. Women think it's a good time to talk intimate. "But men are much more compartmentalized—to men, sex is sex and talk is talk," says sex therapist Sheila Jackman, director of division of human sexuality at the Albert Einstein College of Medicine in New York City.

A situation may be there when a discussion gets overheated. Sometimes it starts with the rearranging of furniture in the living room and descends into a nasty match over your tastes and values. When the arguments are getting directed at the other person than the issue, it's time to drop the issue, to cool down.

One way to withdraw from a discussion that's turned both vicious and silly, says Martin Goldberg, M.D., director of Marriage Council of Philadelphia, is to device an agreed-upon signal to "drop it". "The point is to have a non-debatable signal that you can use even if there are other people around," says Dr. Goldberg. "It's a gimmick, but it works." The idea is to give both parties a chance to take a break from it.

Sometimes it's smart to cut short a discussion when you sense that it's leading nowhere; in fact, it's getting counterproductive. "Many women feel that a relationship's working if they can talk about it. But men don't have the same tolerance for discussions—they think the relationship is not working if they have to keep talking about it," cautions Deborah Tannen, in her book *You Just Don't Understand: Women and Men in Conversation.*

In many marital situations of potential conflict, silence perhaps has an edge over speech. There is wisdom in not talking—in shelving acrimonious issues or simply shutting up sometimes. It has always to be remembered that few issues are as important as the marriage relationship itself.

One Secret of Happy Marriage: Separate Bathrooms

When Charles Watts of *Rolling Stones* was asked the secret of his happy marriage, he replied "separate bathrooms".

Indeed, a husband can do better by using a separate room for keeping his clothes and dressing up. If nothing else, he can press the spare guestroom into service—perforce to be shared with the guest when there's one. In effect, he uses the master bedroom (still carrying the sexist nomenclature) strictly as a bedroom. And restricts his use of the attached bathroom to nightly emergencies.

That way he leaves his mate an almost autonomous zone for bathing, dressing, and various other intimate matters women are supposed to attend to. Such personal space is all the more welcome to her if she's seeing too much of him otherwise, like his happening to work at home.

A well-appointed bathroom all to oneself is a real luxury. You don't have to "adjust" to the convenience of anyone else. A place where you're with yourself, undisturbed, unhurried. You can spread out all your stuff, and there's none to pry into or interfere with the arrangement. And whether you clean it immediately after use or leave it in a mess is entirely your own business.

Bathrooms that way are a private world. Well, if you want to know the truth about other people, their bathroom possibly gives out better clues than the living room—of their habits and hopes, illnesses and hang-ups, even bits of sex life stand revealed in that small room.

One common source of contention between couples sharing a bathroom: the one who had gone there before had left it messier. Husbands generally labour under a genuine belief, their use of the bathroom is tidier, based on the premise their ablutions are seemingly simpler. Even otherwise, many a man rates himself tidier than his mate in matters of hygiene.

Wives routinely complain it falls to their lot to wipe things clean—the tub, the washbasin, the toilet seat, even the floor after their men have been through. And mostly it's the man who is the first user of a shared bathroom—possibly not a bad arrangement otherwise, with men averaging less time in bathrooms than women.

And, of course, there's the perennial complaint of husbands neglecting to lift the seat every time they urinate. In Sweden, some feminist groups have started advocating, men should adapt the practice of urinating sitting down. To which a few men have been known to retort, "To urinate standing is possibly the only male privilege left."

The scene at the breakfast table should spell far more harmony where a working couple assembles after having used separate bathrooms—and separate dressing places—for getting ready. "The critical period in matrimony is breakfast," says A. P. Herbert, a noted writer. Similarly, with separate bathrooms and dressing places, one can visualize a less contentious scenario when a couple is getting ready for an evening party.

Admittedly this arrangement of separate bathrooms calls for some sacrifice on the part of the hubby; forsaking the dwelling's best bathroom for something less elegant. Yet the gains in spousal goodwill could far outweigh the foregone comfort and convenience.

The bathroom is no longer simply a utility space, poorly lit, with leaky taps and wet cement floor. The family bathroom is fast becoming a place where, while doing your business, you can stay relaxed, savour the surroundings, even think out things. The whole approach to home bathrooms has been undergoing a steady change, with emphasis on more space, pleasing décor, superior fittings, water-spillage control, and bright lighting.

Architects are designing bathrooms with lots of white and large floor-to-ceiling mirrors. The standard small tiles are giving way to wide slabs, coloured or printed. Floors are usually equipped with fluffy, non-slip, water-proof carpeting. Funds and space permitting, some are being fitted with a corner jacuzzi unit.

The wonted bathroom now has a large, deep enamel tub, a separate shower section, and twin wash basins, with the lavatory unit isolated. The ubiquitous bathroom scales give an always accurate reading. Extra care is taken to put in attractive cabinets that are roomy and convenient to use.

With busy people, a workday morning often means a quick shower rather than a leisurely bath.

Ideally, a shower should be an enclosed square, about 4 ft on every side. And the cabin should have a door, preferably a glass door, not just a curtain. One should be able to close the door with some assurance that no matter whatever you do in there, no water would leak out onto the bathroom floor.

There's now a place to put the soap where it's out of the line of water spray. A soggy soap is a sure irritant.

The shower should shoot a heavy stream of water at your body, not a faint scattered spray. Better if the nozzle is easily adjustable all the way from a dense, hose-like hit to a wide spray.

And water should be coming under controlled temperature. Indeed, the controls should not only be easy to manipulate but clear enough to be identified by an average myopic minus glasses. It isn't at all amusing to be hit with a stream of scalding hot water or suffering an icy spray.

Showering is surely quicker and somewhat more hygienic, yet there are certain things possible in a tub you just can't do in a shower: to lie soaked, to read, or to sip a drink.

Dynamics of the Double Bed

Theoretically, marriage is all about 'two persons becoming one'. But in the real world, they are not one; they're two, and there's only so far two persons can conceivably blend.

Take the double bed, the quintessential mark of marriage. It's a real challenge to find cozy room for four arms and legs—arms and legs that demanded no special space all day.

The most challenging complication is the common cover.

According to some medical specialists, the male and female of the human species are biologically quite dissimilar in their temperature requirements. Women have protective layers of fat against cold and a built-in thermostat that produces less body heat in summer. Men are prone to suffer more, both from cold and heat.

Even the sleep requirements of the two are different. The average man, often doing more demanding physical work, needs more sleep than his mate.

Snoring presents its own problems. Men snore louder than women, and alcohol intake steps up that roar. Wives too troubled by a mate's snoring are known to shift their pillow to the foot of the double bed—a move viewed by the other party as "unfriendly". This does put some five feet of distance—instead of the usual foot—between her ears and the source of the noise.

Sharing a bed is therefore a complex, changing, even a challenging experience. Paul Rosenblatt, a professor of social sciences at the University of Minnesota, has written a book *Two in a Bed: the Social System of Couple Bed Sharing*. He found that for most couples chatting in bed was the best time they had talking to each other, something that helped their relationship. Couples not talking at this time is an indicator of a troubled marriage.

During Rosenblatt's queries, many respondents did concede that they would possibly get better sleep in separate beds. Yet they found the shared bed more advantageous. Particularly, women feel a sense of security, having another protective body alongside.

The double bed is a multipurpose arena, and it's important that the two parties specify which activity they're undertaking after the Conversation Curfew.

"Are we seeing TV, or are we reading?"

"Are we not talking because of some sulk, or because we both just don't feel like talking?"

"Are we sleeping, or are we fooling around?"

The good thing about marriage is that there is less pressure to make any given night magical. You always know you can have another shot tomorrow, and the next night.

Possibly the greatest virtue of the double bed is its role as a breach healer. Most marriage rows spring from little things; a small complaint here, a slight refusal there, one partner's feelings are hurt, the other goes into a sulk. The man hurries up his tooth-brushing, gets into his night clothes, and plunks down on the farthest edge of his bed. Draws up the cover over his head and almost peevishly turns his back on his soul mate. She, with a longer nightly toilet routine, later slides into hers.

It's a long time before the two actually fall asleep, the man usually the first. Till then, each keeps on thinking ruefully, "Why not end this silly quarrel? Why not snuggle in besides the partner; no doubt erring but still loved?" But who's to make the first crucial move, to "eat crow"? They often end up having a restive night. And so they remain quite in a mood next day to nurse more grievances, real or imagined.

In beds separated by night tables, it means crossing that horrid chasm of three feet. Even in joined beds, any conciliatory move has to be telegraphed; the "magnanimous" partner shuffling out of covers and tugging at those of the partner.

This deliberate gesture takes some doing.

In a double bed, things are apt to turn out easier. A tentative toe stretched towards the centre. Quite by accident it touches a leg. There's no real obligation to withdraw the toe. So it stays. Maybe, it's rewarded by a gentle return pressure. The underlying yearning for amity begins to flow. A hand by chance may brush a side. Heads draw near, arms may reach out. . . The physical contact has broken the ice, even if no formal reconciliation results before falling asleep.

The Wife's Birthday

"I just don't like fuss on my birthday," I say, as I am persuading the good wife to cancel her plans of inviting a dozen friends to dinner.

A little peeved she says, "Me, I like a fuss on my birthday. On that day, I expect a nice present and a shower of attention. No sort of reciprocity going there; if you don't like your birthday, that's your problem."

And she gets the fuss, as I dote on her. Indeed, over 30 years of marriage, the whole thing has developed into an elaborate ritual.

A birthday card chosen with much care. For some years I've taken to the bizarre practice of giving two birthday cards, as if the writing on one wouldn't be conveying enough. Flowers: roses, red, 20. Maybe it's time to introduce an element of surprise here. And one-kg bitter chocolate cake with the birthday inscription. These are all secreted in the evening before.

The ceremonial begins with the bed tea, served in our best china.

Quite often a few close relatives are invited at breakfast for the birthday cake ritual and photographs. The idea is to spring this gathering as a surprise on her but every time the news leaks out.

And then an intimate dinner at a pricey place. Often I opt for Bokhara in Mauraya; a lively eatery where food, more so the tandoori fare, rarely disappoints.

Back home for a brandy, and if the mood is on, the horizontal position. A fitting finale to another "attentive" birthday.

Lately, funds permitting, I take her out of Delhi for a few days. The venue may be different but the drill for the day is nearly the same. Last year at Kandy, Sri Lanka, the hotel management put up an impressive complimentary cake at breakfast. As portions of the same were distributed to strangers sitting on other tables, there were nods and smiles all around. A couple of them even ventured to give a peck to the birthday lady. And when we returned to our room at night, we found the bed decked with rose petals in a heart-shaped formation, as if we were newly married. It's a memorable birthday, mumbled the lady.

Men and women seem to package the reality of birthdays differently. In our achievement-oriented times, men may find themselves wanting. They don't want to go through another one of those stock-taking periods. While some virtually dread their birthdays, others show singular lack of enthusiasm for the occasion.

Women, on the other hand, are typically excited about birthdays and anniversaries. They anticipate such symbolic occasions with pleasure. The so-called anniversary effects tend to be positive for them. And God help you if you ever forget your wife's birthday. "The best way to remember your wife's birthday is to forget it once," says a wit.

In a large American study on psychological factors in mortality, it came out that an approaching birthday seemed to prolong life in women and precipitate death in men. The study, based on 2.7 million deaths from natural causes, found that women were more likely to die in the week after their birthdays than in any other week during the year, whereas men tended to die shortly before their birthdays.

Possibly the trickiest part of birthday and anniversary celebrations is the giving of gifts. There is really no substitute to serious thinking and planning if you want to give a memorable gift. The time and energy spent in selection forms significant part of the gift. Little wonder, people have begun giving cash instead of articles; that saves them the bother of thinking. And in these inflationary times, the cash looks more impressive than what it could buy. But you simply can't give cash to your wife on her birthday; she has most of your money anyway.

Giving and Receiving of Gifts

We're into the season of gift-giving and gift-receiving.

The hunger for gifts is a "hunger for approval, importance, affection and love," says Dawn Bryan, author of *The Art and Etiquette of Gift Giving*. And she adds that to the extent women are insecure in these areas, gifts assume a loaded significance. Men who have traditionally enjoyed greater economic status don't see gift-giving as so important and vital.

Women tend to make a big deal out of gifts, men don't. Again women retain long memories about gifts. Men generally shrug off the experience of receiving a dud.

Here, one is not talking of the increasingly elaborate and expensive gifts given by businesses in the garb of Diwali, Xmas and New Year greetings; it's about gifts among relatives and friends.

And possibly no gift-giving area is as tricky as the exchange of gifts between couples, especially on birthdays and marriage anniversaries. Gift-giving between couples can easily backfire.

Husbands have an in-built tendency to gift useful objects—things, they think, will make the life of their mate easier, such as a microwave oven or a vacuum cleaner. But for wives nothing equals a gift of jewellery (including a trendy watch), with a silk sari far down as the second best. As for perfumes, women often prefer to select and buy these on their own.

A holiday trip is an excellent gift. But then it still has to be supplemented by a gift article.

One theory why so many gifts from husbands go awry is that, men learn about gifts from their mothers, and these lessons stick on for a long time. Mothers are easily gratified with any gifts—a pair of slippers or a bread cutter—from their teenage kids. Wives expect more imaginative, more memorable gifts. And not only must a gift impress the recipient, in some circles it must stand the scrutiny of finicky friends. It's like show-and-tell. "What did he give you for the marriage anniversary or your birthday?" is a question commonly asked.

One wife who has been getting good gifts advises like this. "Accept all his gifts. For the first couple of years these may be awful, but don't say so or you'll scare him off. He'll stop giving you things. If you're enthusiastic, he'll get better with time. Giving gifts between couples is like sex; if you stick with it, it gets better, and a cheerful response over time encourages better performance. If gifts are offers of love, they often demand the greatest act of love in return—refraining from saying what exactly you think."

That brings us to the intriguing subject of gift-taking. The task of a gift receiver often demands great resources of tact and indulgence. We've all gotten gifts on occasions that would strain the patience of a saint.

Possibly one should accept gifts the way a prima dancer receives flowers at the end of a performance, without looking at them too closely and taking them as her due. Some people have this talent. They are a pleasure to give to.

A gift tells us what kind of a person our relatives and friends imagine us to be—wearer of stylish clothes, good with gadgets, lover of books, fond of bric-a-brac. Gifts that fail to address our complexity are potentially unpleasing.

Our gifts parody people; we treat women too exaggeratedly as women, and men too much as men. Husbands are gifted electric shavers they never use; women are routinely given bottles of perfume.

A memorable present would speak to that elusive entity, the secret self. Because the secret self is hard to find, gift givers concentrate on the self's more obvious parts. A golfer gets golf balls. A dandy gets silk scarves, and a drinking man, bottles of Scotch.

10

What Mars a Marriage!

How do Men and Women Change in Marriage?

Men and women change in marriage. They often change in ways that make the romance go out of their marriage. Indeed, sometimes the woman wonders whether this is the same man she was once married to, while her husband wonders where is the woman he was once smitten with.

Wives have quite a few complaints to make. Husbands stop touching them except for sex. The male approach is understandable. Becoming privy to full sexual favours—the ultimate in touching—his impulse for affectionate touching grows fainter. By instinct, a male is tuned to touch only as a prelude to sex.

Yet nonsexual touch retains its prime importance for a woman. It boosts her self-esteem; experts claim a woman touched several times a day experiences high self-esteem. An affectionate touch is something her body actually craves for. No wonder a woman's skin is ten times more sensitive to touch than a man's.

Once a husband is aware of his mate's sensual need for nonsexual touching, he could be more motivated to please her with the same. She, on her part, should show evident appreciation whenever he touches her in affection, even encouraging him in doing so in non-demanding ways.

Incidentally, wives often complain that men are too hurried and too rough in their touching. This is not to say that there aren't times when a quick or firm touch isn't appropriate, but most of the time, touching has to be soft and unhurried.

Another complaint: husbands stop giving compliments. "He no longer compliments me on a nice dress or a new hairdo; not even an admiring glance when I look my best," rues a wife. A woman, whose body alters noticeably with years, needs lots of reassurance that her partner still finds her appealing.

To a lot of men this doesn't make much sense. A typical response: "I married her because she was beautiful. And she knows my feelings. But what's the point of my reminding her repeatedly of it." The shift does not take place because he doesn't love her, but because he doesn't realize that the action of noticing her and paying compliments means so much to her.

The situation possibly calls for some initiative on the part of wives, too. They should keep on asking husbands how they look, and remind them to say complimentary things. In course of time, their men may get tuned to giving admiring looks and compliments without any prodding.

And then the complaint that husbands stop pursuing them. "Mohan used to find me when he came home from the office," says Reena. "Now straightway he heads for TV or plays with the kids. I don't feel wanted as before." Mohan, like many men, has attained his goal with marriage and so stopped pursuing—the automatic hunter reflex to stop pursuing when you have bagged the quarry.

It seems a good idea to give your wife your first attention on return from work, before settling down to other things. Of course, there are days when one is under considerable stress from work and needs some time alone to recover, yet this practice of giving the first fifteen minutes—the golden minutes—to your mate can reap you rich dividends of her goodwill.

Wives voice a common lament: husbands stop talking to them, even stop listening to them. On their part, men usually assert that they remain silent because there is nothing important to say.

With women, it's different. The calm men achieve through silence, women usually achieve through talking. To women the very process of conversation with their partners boosts rapport. They experience greater intimacy by sharing thoughts and feelings.

Some wives are particularly piqued because their husbands are not silent by nature but mostly stay mum with them. "He seems to have everything to say to everyone else, and nothing to say to me," moans one.

A man listening to his mate encounters a peculiar difficulty. Mere listening is too inactive for him; he's always inclined to offer solutions. But often an upset woman—say, upset over some skin problems—is not looking for solutions; she simply feels better when listened to with sympathetic attention.

"You're not listening." The use of this expression is a complete turn-off for a man. He feels frustrated because he is usually listening in some way, or at least trying to. Even if he was not, the phrase jars on him; in childhood it was used repeatedly by his mother in admonishing him.

Wives can make their men do much more for them if they showed appreciation every time he did something, big or small. Even show appreciation for house help he is otherwise supposed to render.

Coping with Clutter

An American Clutter Clinic counseling people on how to get rid of things: "If you haven't touched it, worn it, sat on it, or smelled it in the last two years, then get rid of it." A woman laughed when she heard this first and said, "You just described my husband."

An affluent consumer society collects a lot of clutter. The problem has become so critical in countries in the West that specialist agencies (with names like Conquering Clutter, Clutter Coaching or even Clutter Therapy) have sprung up everywhere. These instruct their clients on stuff-management for their offices and homes.

Most of our world suffers from having too little, much less having homes to clutter up; that way poverty is a sovereign remedy for clutter. But with the burgeoning middle-classes, bitten by the bug of consumerism, we will also be increasingly victims of our possessions.

There was the old-time middle-class clutter, where almost everything was saved for a possible future use, even if it was a piece of string. Then, the things being added for retention were rather few, and the older houses had all those nooks and recesses to take care of that.

The new consumer clutter is vastly different. It pervades the whole house: almirahs and their tops, shelves, boxes, lofts, under the beds, even basements and garages (sometimes as much as pushing the car out). Children are great producers of the stuff in the shape of toys and clothes that they outgrow or no longer want.

Many men are clutter maniacs where paper is concerned. Women seem more prone to the collecting of clothes, and all types of odds and ends. Perhaps they retain more objects for reasons of sentiment or nostalgia. But the kitchen stuff is probably more addictive these days—accumulations of electric mixes and grinders, juice extractors and coffee percolators, and now microwave ovens—while servants mostly continue cooking in their old ways. Some compulsive shopping is inevitable where ownership and acquisition of modern gadgets symbolize advancement and prestige.

The clutter problem was manageable until people started moving into newer block homes, especially flats. Here, storage space is at a premium.

The storage space itself is being utilized more intensively. In the West, a new occupation has emerged—that of the storage or closet specialist. Experts visit customers' homes, assess the requirements and then custom-design hanging and shelving systems. It is typically claimed that in the reorganized closets customers can store twice as much as they could before.

The basic technique is to split a closet's interior into a large number of narrow or short compartments that fit much more closely the height and width used to hang clothes and to store things on shelves.

In the fast-growing consumer culture, it is well-nigh a hopeless task to curtail acquisition, more so of newer things and newer designs and makes. The "clutter coaches" accordingly concentrate attention on the speedy and timely disposal of the accumulated stuff. They recommend regular periodic elimination of possessions and papers, at least once a quarter. The longer it gets delayed, the harder it becomes to organize, the time and effort needed proving too daunting for some.

In disposing, we enjoy a manifest advantage; almost everything second-hand sells, and often fetches an acceptable price. And there are all those "buyers on bicycles" who shout themselves hoarse wanting to buy your stuff at your doorstep, and against ready cash. People perhaps underestimate the crucial role the *kabbadi* plays in the recycling industry, now a major industry.

In the ultimate analysis, staying clutter-free is more a question of attitude and motivation than any expert advice or techniques. Clutter is often the result of indecision or if one is naturally messy.

There is a theory that the tidiness of your home reflects the state of your marital relationship. A neat household, it is argued, is a sign of marital harmony whereas a messy one signals an uneasy relationship. Possibly, real trouble arises if one of the partners happens to be either obsessively tidy or hopelessly slovenly.

Clutter is more of a problem where residents of a house live on permanent basis. Those who happen to move around from time to time cannot cart their surplus stuff alongside at every move. To that extent, they remain relatively free of clutter.

The crucial question: can we stop accumulating stuff? For some people, accumulation of stuff satisfies a pathological need—the business of acquiring things, dusting, moving, storing, or keeping track of the collected stuff. That way, clutter narcotizes their sense of purposelessness and imparts to them a feeling of being busy.

So how do we deliver ourselves from our obsession with stuff? There is no dearth of solutions being bandied about; the challenge is figuring out which of them will work, long term, not only for individuals but also for society as a whole.

Dismaying though it may sound, the prospects of reining in consumerism are in no way promising, even more so in developing countries with more and more people caught up with the hunger for consumer goods.

Maybe one concrete measure that could curb consumerism is to de-commercialize our rituals of weddings and of some festivals such as Diwali. Far too many things are bought, used, and gifted away on these occasions. However, even this small step calls for the growth of a countrywide sentiment.

The person who invented the wastepaper basket must be a genius. This simple strategy of placing sturdy baskets in every room can keep the place tidy; removing clutter of wrappers, paper ads and numerous knickknacks. Clearing the wastepaper baskets regularly and keeping them in their accustomed places is one known way of managing clutter.

The Family Slob

Usually in a couple, if one is a zealot for cleaning, the other is a slob; a sensible balance of nature, it seems. Two neat people would only find themselves arguing endlessly over minor matters. On the other hand, if both are slobs, the household would soon be buried in trash.

"I believe that deep down, most neat people have a basic need to be messed up, and that messy people have a similar need to be tidied," says a wit.

The troublesome part; it's mostly the man who is a slob. And it's often a waste of wifely time and energy to reform the slob. If a man has reached the age of thirty without being tidy, the chances of his changing are meagre. (Ideally, if you want to change your man, better have him in his teens, before his mother 'spoils' him.)

A husband left unsupervised can get into all sorts of nasty habits. He'll blow his nose into bed sheets. Deposit his nasal pickings on backs of sofa seats. Pick his teeth with anything that comes to hand—a paper pin, a visiting card. Even pee in the sink.

According to the feminist writer, Sonntag, behaving like a slob is the manifestation of a particularly male primal desire to act "big". Being a slob makes a man bigger because it increases the space he occupies. You often see the husband slumped before TV in his favourite chair with things strewn all around—sandals, cokes, beers, plates of snacks, ashtrays, magazines. And these tend to stay there, till the wife cleans up the mess.

Some women take revenge by outslobbing their husbands or at least not picking up the stuff left by their mates.

In every household one member gets dubbed as the family slob. And this mantle (a bit unfairly, I feel) has fallen on me. At one time our teenage son was a tough contender for the title. His pyjamas would lie the whole day on the same spot where he got out of them in the morning. And such a lot of clutter in his room, you needed utmost caution to step inside—the way you'd negotiate a muddy pavement patch.

I deem myself quite meticulous at the office. Only I do let down my guard at home after a hard day's work.

My closet of clothes is still better organized than those of the wife. I always hang a suit in its cover after use; she just dumps her clothes on shelves. I have seen her close a drawer with a sock half hanging out. And then there's her habit of collecting plastic carrier bags, stuffing them inside other carrier bags, and hanging the whole lot on cupboard knobs.

But what possibly irritates her most is my habit of making a ball of every publicity handbill that flutters out of morning papers and hurling the same from the bed into the corner wastebasket. The success rate is around 30 percent. On Sunday mornings when we get four papers, the area around the waste basket is strewn with paper missiles.

To Nag or Not to Nag

"When his wife nags, the civilized man goes to a club instead of reaching for one," says a wit.

The unflattering stereotype of a nagging wife has persisted through centuries. She's a figure of fun whose one preoccupation is to correct and improve the husband.

Women, men make out, remain engaged in persistent, petty faultfinding as if they are under some compulsion to treat their husbands as kids. "Use your hankie, not the napkin, to blow your nose." "Again, you left your book open upside down." "At yesterday's dinner you started nibbling at your food before all the ladies had been served." "You're overtaking from the wrong side." And the same goes on endlessly.

Of late, a novel development: Some women writers have come up with self-help books cautioning wives against the perils of nagging. Prominent among these publications are *The Surrendered Wife* by Laura Doyle (Simon & Schuster) and *Surrendering to Marriage* by Iris Krasnow (Talk Miramax). Laura Doyle's book, a bestseller, is the most provocative of all:

At first our marriage (she married at 22) was blissful. Then, I started to see John's imperfections more glaringly, and I began correcting him. It was my way to helping him improve. From my point of view, if he could just be more ambitious at work, more romantic at home, and clean up after meals, everything would be fine. I told him as much. He didn't respond well. ...The harder I pushed the more he resisted, and we both grew irritable and frustrated.

This is how Doyle starts her book. When none of her "mothering" and nagging changed her husband, she changed herself, becoming a "surrendered wife". She stopped finding fault with his driving—conceding he had been driving all right for years before marriage. She stopped instructing him on what to wear. And let him manage his own health. She even avoided giving him a disapproving look; husbands are so familiar with their wives' body language that they can easily read a scowl. All in all, it meant treating her husband as an intelligent adult rather than an irresponsible youngster.

To feminists, nagging is a male word and a way of debasing female speech. Women, being conditioned to be effective in matters of detail, can't help pointing out when their men are found wanting.

A nagging wife is often an indication that the man of the house is inconsiderate or lousy. Hasn't it been rightly said that a man who has faults he doesn't know about probably doesn't listen to his wife—because she is the person who knows him best in the world.

Conceded, women may be doing more than their fair share of nagging but men nag, too; in their case it's more like bullying. Conceited men actually prove to be the worst naggers.

Indeed, the popular notion that women are natural naggers is more of a myth. Just because wives keep reminding husbands of what they should be doing, their talk is construed as nagging. Feminists anyway make out that nagging isn't natural to women; it's a consequence of women's subordinate position in society. Having less power than men, women at times have to nag out of necessity.

Nagging as a way of self-assertion by either party can remain a light-hearted affair if indulged in private. The problems start when it's done in front of others, even one's children.

And a good nag is plainly preferable to a mountainous sulk.

To nag or not to nag? That's the question on which the final word has still to be said.

In Defence of the Marital Sulk

One of the most gratifying options in ventilating a marital grievance is to sulk, a sort of *satyagraha* in the wedded world. And a satyagraha, as Gandhiji, its fountainhead postulated, "May be offered to one's nearest and dearest".

You can actually nurture a sulk with dignity. And the best part; you can slip out of it when you wish. You don't have to await an apology from the guilty party; you simply stop moping, behave like a normal spouse again.

You don't have to be a wife to sulk; husbands can sulk as well. Yet wives, one imagines, must be experiencing far more occasions to sulk: the hubby turning up unduly late from work without the courtesy of a phone call, or bringing along somebody for dinner without as much as prior notice. But wives have this problem; it's their lot to ensure that the wheels of the household run smoothly. It sometimes makes them forget that they are in the midst of a well-deserved sulk.

A sulk can be anything from a half-hour affair to a fully forty-eight-hour sulk. It's akin to emotional strike action; you still function as a spouse but you work to rule. The underlying message in sulking is the hurt you feel, because the other party has acted so selfishly or thoughtlessly.

Retiring to another room or staying out of sight does no good to a sulk; the other party might forget you are nursing one. However, it is important to avoid eye contact. An inadvertent smile can damage a sulk irreparably. That's the ironclad rule of sulk: once you have un-sulked you can't re-sulk.

What's better for marital peace; silence or speech? Not an easy question to answer. Communication is the buzzword these days. To its votaries, every problem—political, social, and marital—arises out of poor communication among the participants. Marriage counselors are extolling the rewards of communication and marriage manuals sing its virtues.

For some time past, sulking had gone out of favour. Couples were advised to vent their feelings. The whole theory was to let the rancour flow, instead of being bottled up. Books came up with titles like *It's Fun to be Furious* and *The Happy Hollerer*. But now sulks have staged a comeback, and for cogent reasons. Yet one is not sure whether the communication mantra—good for the boardroom—is always productive in the bedroom.

Surely, the way to solve problems in married life is to talk them out. Yet couples tuned to over-communicating (to votaries of communication, there is not such a thing as overdoing communication) are often seen making use of verbal weapons camouflaged as "reasonable discussions"—phrases which are seemingly polite but actually barbed. "Forgive me if I say" is one. "I've my faults but you ..." is another. Such verbal game-play can end up more in frayed tempers than an increased understanding of each other's point of view. It's communication all right but of the most invidious variety. Some modern couples seem to be perilously good at it.

Sulking, with its studied silence, may well have an edge over instant speech in many a marital situation. "If you don't talk, you don't fight" is an old adage. "Silence is one of the hardiest arguments to refute," says John Billings.

A sulk anyway gives a couple time enough to develop an altered perspective and an opportunity to separate what is vital from what is not, before words fly out like arrows—missiles that can't be recalled. In the meantime, the routine of daily living should begin to soften the hurt that gave rise to the sulk.

In defence of the marital sulk, the offending party gets the message while no harsh words are bandied about. The only risk: a sulkier starting to enjoy the attention the sulk evokes from the sulked—things like little acts of help, even an admission of guilt or selfishness.

Forgetful Husbands

"Do pick up my saree from Snowhite on your way back from office," says Savita.

"Sure," replies Ranjit, watching cricket on TV.

But when he returns home next day, he has forgotten to collect the saree.

"Don't forget it tomorrow," says Savita in an irritated vein.

And, lo, next day again Ranjit forgot to bring it. He's genuinely sorry for the lapse.

Savita is exasperated. She just can't understand how Ranjit, a considerate husband otherwise, forgets such a simple errand when he can remember numerous minute details of his managerial job.

To wives, this phenomenon of forgetful husbands is well-nigh baffling. Why men forget while women remember? It can't be all the pressure of work. Working women, operating under similar pressure, rarely forget any of the umpteen household chores.

One explanation is that in the male instinctual priority, household chores figure far lower than work-related tasks. And there, again, things that aren't instinctually male get missed more often. Collecting the laundry or picking some foodstuff run a greater chance of getting forgotten than, say, repairs to the family car or fixing a leaky faucet.

Men, it seems, are mainly focused on their work, despite a growing inclination on their part to be of help at home. And the more focused a man is on his work or more stressed with it, his tendency to forget domestic details rises.

This tendency is most marked in married men. Apparently, as the wife begins to remember more and more of household details, the husband starts remembering them less and less. The more she worries, the less he worries. Surely the wife can't be blamed for this development but her behaviour does have an impact on what the man forgets.

How to make him remember? Nagging or getting angry over such memory lapses proves rather unproductive. And so also the oft-repeated charge: "You weren't listening". That may actually be incorrect; he did listen but forgot. The more his woman nags, the more he's apt to forget what he was asked to do.

Marriage counselors and psychiatrics have been putting forth a flurry of suggestions. But possibly the best advice for wives comes from John Gray in his book *What Your Mother Couldn't Tell You and Your Father Didn't Know* (Vermillion).

According to Gray, a man forgets a request when it is conveyed in a negative way. The forgotten request, however, is not completely lost. It is just stored in a different place. With a little help from his mate, he can automatically remember what he normally forgets.

Gray advocates advanced relationship skills for wives which, carried over a period of time, can reap them enormous benefits. And here he emphasizes two particular points.

Every time you ask your man to do a thing, ask as if for the first time. The tone of your voice is very important. Behave as if you have completely overlooked his earlier omissions to do the thing despite being asked twice or thrice. Such behaviour comes most pleasing to the man. A refreshing change for one who was apprehending a whining complaint or an angry argument.

Each time a man forgets to do something, and his wife reacts in a non-demanding way, he will suddenly remember all the times he has forgotten. It is amazing. If she does not remind him of how many times she had to ask, then he remembers all on his own. His memory for doing the little day-to-day things is strengthened when he's getting reminded without having to feel guilty.

Gray's recipe looks clearly irksome, especially to start with. It calls for much self-control and patience on the wife's part, to be practiced over months or longer till it becomes a part of her marital skills. But then she is only extending it to her loved one. And the gains in his goodwill and cooperation are enormous.

The other point he makes out is the man's perennial hunger for appreciation. The secret of getting more from a man is to appreciate what he is already doing and then ask for more in small increments.

So it makes an excellent strategy for the wife to show her appreciation, by word or smile, whenever her mate does anything in the house, big or small. She should always behave as if he has done a favour, though it may well be expected of him. Over the time, as a man experiences that his doing small things is so well appreciated by his mate and brings her happiness, he remembers to do more and more of them.

Are You Listening?

The complaint most often voiced by wives: the husband is not listening. Dissatisfaction with the way their husbands listen to them stems on two counts.

Firstly, they don't find their husbands giving the requisite conversational responses in the shape of verbal interjections or even looking at the speaker. This could leave a wife with the uncomfortable feeling she hadn't been fully heard—often making her go through the motions of repeating herself. She expects "supportive" interruptions and matching body language, all indicative of his interest in what she's saying. What she may actually get is an occasional grunt while the man is rifling through magazines or staring at the tube. He may well be listening but she could never tell the same from his demeanour.

The second grouse is that a husband often times fails to remember what he has been told; he simply "tunes out".

Seema told Rajesh, there was a party at Pandeys on the coming Saturday. He said, "Fine." Seema took care to remind him of the same on Saturday morning as he was going for golf—the extra precaution she's gotten used to taking.

Around seven that evening, she sees Rajesh sprawled before the TV watching Wimbledon. "It's time to get dressed. We've got to go." Rajesh looks puzzled. "Go? Where are we going?" he asks. "You never listen to me," she retorts in exasperation.

Rajesh, and husbands like him, seem to be suffering from a physical handicap that could be classified as Selective Deafness or Husband Hearing Impairment. This state of affairs infuriates wives no end.

A husband may make light of this handicap by saying, "I know you will tell me again, anyway." But then if she reminds him too often, that could constitute nagging.

Most men, it looks, are not tuned to patient listening unless someone is supplying "useful" information or they have to listen to someone in a position of power. When a wife's talk doesn't happen to fall in these two categories, it is apt to secure scant attention, especially between couples who have been married a long time.

Laura Stafford, a communication expert, advances a somewhat comforting theory about marital conversation. According to her, letting your wife's or husband's words go in one ear and out the other, isn't as damaging to marriage as is commonly feared. In fact, it's the sign of a stable, happy marriage. Only in the early stages of wedlock you listen closely to your spouse. You are evaluating your partner, forming impressions. This phase is mostly over within a decade or two of marriage.

Thurber, the famed American humorist, counseled husbands as to how they can "listen" to their wives without listening. (Mind, though, that his advice came in the days before television—and feminism.)

"The best way of dealing with a wife who tells long stories of the day's happenings, or reads accounts of murders aloud when her husband has settled down to his book or journal, is to pretend to listen but not really listen at all. ...

This form of deception is, of course, fairly easy to practice when the female is reading aloud, for her eyes must naturally be upon the printed page before her. It is not so easy when she is relating an occurrence, or a chain of occurrences, for her eyes are then likely to be upon the male. In this case he should contrive, as soon as she begins, to drop his magazine or newspaper on his knee, as if he had abandoned it—all the time, however, keeping the type within range.

A defense against forward passes, as they say in football, must also be carefully built by the inattentive husband. By forward passes, I mean sudden and unexpected questions which the wife is likely to fling at any moment. ... Each particular husband, knowing the twists and turns of his particular wife's mind, must work out his own system of defense against forward passes."

That's the classic scene of conversational disaccord among couples when they meet at home after work. To women, exchange of confidences and bits of information is an important part of getting closer. Men believe they remain silent because there is nothing important to say. (The argument that the man may be more tired after work is not convincing enough; the woman who works could be tired, too.)

Husbands: An Irritating Form of Life

The irritations these creatures cause constitute a long list.

At parties, you may see them dutifully handing chairs to their wives and bringing them drinks. But when not with other people around, husbands are apt to ignore all minor courtesies.

A husband stays calm and cool about the ailments of his spouse. But if he himself gets a sniffle of cold or an upset tummy, he thinks he's about to perish. Moans aloud for his mamma, while expecting full attention from his wife.

They always swallow alcoholic drinks faster than they can assimilate them. And perceive themselves as martyrs if the wife gives as much as a disapproving look.

They are quite energetic in walking miles on a golf course. But if it's doing anything in the house they feign fatigue, grow lethargic.

Husbands forget anniversaries and birthdays. They can well forget a dinner date if engrossed in watching their favourite sport on TV.

And they forget to carry out simple requests of their mates. To women, this phenomenon of forgetful husbands is well-nigh baffling—husbands who as office executives can remember a host of complex matters but as householders forget elementary chores. Nagging or jogging his memory by getting angry is known to prove counter-productive.

A husband's touch with bottle openers is sure and steady. But he's apt to fumble if asked to help the wife in loosening a stuck necklace clasp.

In minutes after his head hits the pillow, a husband could be snoring like an overloaded bus, more so if he had a few drinks inside him.

And he cannot so much as wash his face without splashing water all over the basin.

Indeed, men turn into slobs once they are married. They belch deliberately in front of their families, and let out loud farts unashamedly. They pick their teeth with anything that comes to hand.

To many wives, their partners turn into near infants after some years of marriage—mere eating, sleeping and expelling machines who bawl loudly if their dinner is late by as much as ten minutes.

And most husbands stay buoyed with the belief that when they have been particularly remiss, they can cure everything with a big kiss.

Many wives start with the thinking they can correct their husbands' faults through pointing these out. But they soon learn about the futility of that exercise. Every time they do so, he brings forth a maddeningly logical explanation of his transgression. Or he puts on a look of such melancholy that it's the wife, instead of him, who starts feeling the remorse of the transgressor. Actually each time he transgresses, the wife's chances of correcting his faults grow less.

And yet, through some quirk of Providence, many men manage to stay deeply ensconced in the affection of their mates.

Nobody as yet has figured out what exactly women can do to improve husbandly behaviour. But for men, the American poet Ogden Nash has this advice in his poem *A Word To Husbands.*

To keep your marriage brimming,
With love in the loving cup,
Whenever you're wrong, admit it,
Whenever you're right, shut up.

Couples in Cars

If there's any time in married life when couples are apt to have a row, it is while out in their cars. "The small enclosed space of a car is a powerful symbol that you're together," says Dr. Isaiah Zimmerman, an American couples' therapist.

Complicating the balance of power between couples is the fact that within the confines of a car, the person behind the wheel has the upper hand. This usually arouses the other sitting alongside to redress the imbalance by making "helpful" suggestions in driving.

"Mind the scooter on the left." "Watch that fool wobbling on his bicycle." "Give way to the fellow hooting behind." Bina continues her backseat driving while sitting on the front seat.

At times, Vivek wishes he would have a car fitted with dual controls, the ones favoured by driving schools. "Better do it yourself," he could then say, and take his hands off the steering wheel and his feet off the peddles. Vivek clearly nurses the belief that men are born with a good driving gene that women lack.

That is why the situation turns trickier when a wife is driving and the husband is "idly" sitting by.

Looking into Delhi traffic conditions, your best bet is that if you can afford it, hire a chauffeur so you can sit relaxed in the back seat.

Our world, it seems, is peopled with badly-driven wives—almost as aggrieved as battered wives. And while the beaten wife may have had a hand in provoking the assault, the victim of the husband-lousy-driver syndrome is invariably the innocent party.

"Mine—otherwise a manageable man—turns a macho the moment he gets behind the wheel. Overtakes most alarmingly. Mishaps are missed by inches, giving me a fright every time. But what worries me more: a hit may result in a fight."

"Mine's the exact reverse", says another. "Chugs along at his leisurely pace in the old Fiat. It was all right in Jaipur but is proving a virtual nightmare in Delhi. Impatient Hondas honk at us and buses bear us down. Even auto rickshaws want to overtake us. I'm often left pressing an imaginary accelerator."

"Mine is a horror," a third confides, "when driving after drinking at a party. His eyesight, otherwise not too good, worsens with a few whiskies. The other night we nearly overran a cyclist. I have really to act as a co-pilot. Tell him at times that the green light ahead was for the straight traffic, not for us turning right."

"Mine," adds one more, "has developed this awful habit of cursing every erring driver in sight. The continuous diatribe gets on my nerves."

Yet possibly the most heated exchanges erupt when couples driving to an unknown destination are trying to find their way.

Men are mostly reluctant to ask for directions despite repeated urgings from their mates. To men, it pricks their pride to seek outside help; to wives its plain male obstinacy. A couple looking for a house that is hosting a dinner party could become so bitterly argumentative, they may simply give up the search, and end up eating an omlette at home in stony silence, dressed in party clothes.

Surely cars are not all trouble for couples. An automobile can also create a cocoon of intimacy. "I love taking long drives with Rommi," says Gita. "We put on music, make rambling conversation and feel like we're newly married." Ravi, on his part, finds the rolling of wheels on the asphalt soothing. "It's much easier for me to open up when we're on the road. Maybe it's because part of my brain is occupied with driving, but things come out of my mouth that I could never say across the table." Of course, all this assumes fine driving conditions.

And couples can be happy driving in silence. "Couples are sometimes appalled that they're totally silent during a long drive," says Dr Zimmerman. "You don't have to converse to prove you're a happy couple. Sometimes, you just want to daydream or watch the scenery."

11

Dealing with Our Differences

Here comes some more food for thought from the banquet that is marriage, full of variety but containing some staple items that every couple can recognize.

How Muzzled are the Married?

When living married, you can't leave the house without saying where you're going. You can't not say what time you'll return. Without informing, you can't stay out past midnight, or eleven, or dinnertime. You can't go to parties alone. You can't make plans without consulting the other person, particularly not for the evenings or weekends.

In her book *From Against Love: A Polemic* (Pantheon), Laura Kipnis draws a long list of things that married people can't do on their own.

Here's a small sample from her observations on the marital muzzle:

- **You can't** be a slob. You can't leave your books, tissues, shoes, socks, mail, underwear, office files, or porn lying around the house.
- **You can't** drink straight from the jug or bottle. You can't make crumbs without wiping them up (now, not later). You can't throw wet clothes into the laundry basket.
- **You can't** leave the bathroom door open; it's offensive. You can't leave the bathroom door closed, the other person may need to get in. You can't leave the toilet seat up.

And, of course, as a male you must lift the seat before urinating.

- **You're not allowed** to pay no attention to things you may tend to ignore: your own nose hair, your underarm hair, or your toenails.
- **You can't** sleep apart. You can't fall asleep on the sofa without getting woken up to go to bed. You can't eat in bed. You can't leave bed right away after sex. If you drink milk before sleeping, you can't do without rinsing the glass at sleeping or rising time. You can't turn the air conditioner as high as you want.
- **You can't** work when you're supposed to be relaxing. You can't spend too much time on the computer. You can't e-mail flirtation, however innocent. You can't be rude to people who call on phone for the spouse. And you're not allowed to read when your mate is talking to you—unless you have mastered the art of glancing at newspaper headlines while looking at your mate.
- **You can't** make major purchases alone, or spend money on things the other person considers excesses. You can't have secrets about money (or anything else).
- **You can't** eat what you want. You can't skip meals. You can't eat alone. You can't eat butter if your cholesterol is being monitored. You can't blow your nose at the table. You can't read the newspaper at meals. You can't eat things that give you gas. You can't drink without the other person counting your drinks.
- **You can't** forget things and then go back to the house for them once the door is closed. You can't drive too fast, or faster than the mate defines as fast. You may not criticize the other person's driving, signaling, or lane-changing habits. You can't get angry while driving, or swear at other drivers.
- **You can't** repeat yourself. You can't be overly dramatic. You can't know things the other person doesn't know, or appear to parade your knowledge. You can't begin a sentence with "You always." You can't begin a sentence with "I never."

- **You can't** have the wrong laugh: too loud, too explosive, too inappropriate, too silly. You can't say what you think about the mate's family. You can't compare the mate to any of their family members, especially not the same-sex parent.
- **You can't** talk about past relationships. You can't talk about politics. You can't tell dirty jokes. You can't not 'communicate your feelings.'

In this way, and in hundreds of other ways one can think of, you may keep your marital life harmonious.

A Few Wifely Likes and Dislikes

We like to be kissed. What we love more are surprise kisses—a gift kiss as we are coming out bathed or at the ironing board.

And, mind, a kiss doesn't always need to be a prelude to sex.

We don't like sex when we're in no mood for it. But that doesn't mean we don't like sex most of the time.

We like a man who loves his mother; such a man generally shows respect for women. But we don't want our man talking of his mother all the time.

You don't have to keep repeating "I love you". We prefer to feel the sentiment, to experience "I love you".

We like a well-groomed man, not someone with hair sticking out of his nostrils and ears or with dirty toenails. And there must be spotlessly clean underwear.

When you ask us to accompany you to a party, be more specific about what would be going on and who's going to be there. That way we know what to wear.

A man with shaven pubic hair is no real turn-on; the close-cropped pubic region isn't something exciting to behold. You can surely trim a little off the top and sides but in a manner that doesn't make the whole thing too apparent.

Breasts are great in design and looks, and you should pay periodic attention to them through gazing and fondling. But we aren't terribly enamoured if you focus on breasts all the time, often to the neglect of other regions.

Your efforts at bringing us to an orgasm are greatly appreciated. But this can be overdone. A whole lot of other factors are involved in our orgasm, and these have more to do with us ourselves than with you.

Are Men and Women Getting Mismatched?

Andrew Hacker, a professor at Queens College, New York, has recently written a book *Mismatch: The Growing Gulf between Women and Men*. The distinguished political and social scientist interprets the gender scene as it is evolving in the USA. Yet the same may have some relevance to other societies as well, including ours.

Admittedly, men and women are known to behave differently. They talk differently, they shop differently, they drive differently, they watch TV differently. Their approach to money, sports, politics is different, and so also to personal relationships.

According to Hacker, women and men are moving further apart in virtually every sphere. And he marshals a wealth of statistics and surveys in support of the proposition. The proverbial war between the sexes, he says, has intensified, and shows few signs of abating.

Nowadays women not only expect "full equality", but more and more of them are competing against men. Women reaching parity with men has given rise to quite a few tensions and unresolved issues.

To Hacker, the current high divorce rate (as high as 50 percent in the USA) may be evidence of this estrangement, which transcends the difficulties of individual couples. It's becoming increasingly difficult to describe today's couples as a natural match, the way it was in their grandparents' day, when a natural complementarity between men and women was simply assumed. Men and women were then married to the family, and their marriage reinforced by society, by religion, and so on. There may not have been great sex or continued romance, but the couples learned to live together.

Surely, men and women still live together. But now there's more of a psychological separation; a separation, not just of opinions on various issues, such as crime, schooling, warfare, but also of deeply-held values. Women have a growing consciousness of being their own person.

Hacker attributes the changing gender equation mainly to education; more and more girls going for higher education, and for professions like law and journalism. Men still want to be doctors, but more women are being accepted in medical colleges because they have better records.

Women are often outnumbering men in institutes of higher learning. Some universities in the USA, alarmed at the trend, started giving male applicants extra points to keep gender parity. The practice has been struck down by courts. Yet many schools, even prestigious ones such as Harvard, Yale, and Princeton are said to be letting in men who have lesser records than women, so that they can stay at 50/50.

Many of these women, unwilling to marry down, will have difficulty finding suitable mates.

Based on actual experiments, Hacker finds that his girl students are more reflective than boys. When asked whether the United States was unquestionably the best country in the world, 90 per cent of the boys forthwith said, yes. Only about 60 per cent of girls gave that answer. The rest wanted time to reflect about it.

Similarly, as an exercise in personal relationships, he gave his class, boys and girls, two hours to write down everything they knew about their girlfriend or boyfriend. Twenty minutes later, boys started leaving after having written a couple of pages. Girls were still at it for two hours. Having filled the first book, they were asking for the second.

Has "a new man" arrived on the scene—sensitive, more open to nuances, less authoritarian? Hacker's answer: the "new man" is a fiction. Yes, men are more careful about their language and demeanour. But generally speaking, when you scratch below the surface, you find that men want what their fathers wanted.

Men want the household kept in shape, children looked after, shopping done, and good meals in time. And, by and large, women, even women in two-career marriages, do this for their husbands. She's willing to put much more into it. But then she wants much more from the marriage than her mother or grandmother did. And she does express her disappointment when she doesn't get it.

The odds of a young woman finding Mr. Right or a young man finding Ms. Right are much longer these days, because people have much higher expectations of mates. If not exactly picky, people are getting more selective.

Is the gulf growing between men and women?

Some would accuse Hacker of drawing too flattering a picture of women vis-à-vis men. Men are still staying tops in the corporate world and in politics—the two most competitive areas of human endeavour. They still retain a distinct lead in the money market and the sports field. But then women are progressively closing on the male lead in athletics and sports. Money management is made out to be a mystery—a fertile field for sharpies, when it is something that can easily be learned by anybody with a modest education, if so inclined. Politics, however, needs to be cleaned up a bit before women can participate in the requisite numbers.

Men have to watch their image, especially in the marital arena, if the mismatch is not to grow more ominous. Educated, earning wives, with all the feel of equality, will be harbouring high expectations of their marriage. Hacker is sounding a note of caution to American men, more so American husbands, about the growing gulf between men and women. And this may well apply to men in other countries, including ours.

Shopping: How Different with Women and Men!

Men and women differ in just about every other way—in driving, conversing, laughing, eating, watching TV, handling money or drink. Why shouldn't they be different in shopping?

The conventional wisdom on male shoppers is they don't like to do it, which is why they don't do much of it. And, even when they buy, they rarely shop. Women always shop when they buy, and are estimated to buy 80 percent of everything that is sold.

It's usually a struggle for a woman to get husband as patient company when she shops. Most exchanges between men and women shopping together are more or less bad-tempered. No wonder, a husband often stands outside and watches girls. Big stores and shopping plazas are planning 'crèches' where men can be 'parked', have drinks, snacks and comfortable seats in front of a big-screen TV tuned to sports, while their women shop.

A recent field survey in the UK indicates that shopping in crowded shopping stores raises the stress levels of men to the point it's hazardous to their health. "The peak levels were equivalent to emergency situations experienced by fighter pilots or policemen going into dangerous situations," says British psychologist David Lewis who made a study of men's stress levels at Christmas shopping.

Lewis sent three dozen men and women of different ages to stores with identical Christmas lists. Each shopper was accompanied by a researcher who recorded periodic blood pressure and heart rate. Even before they stepped out the front door, more than 70 percent of men started to show these symptoms. "For men even the thought of going shopping was enough to send stress levels soaring," concludes Lewis.

The stress levels for women who had brought their husbands along were much higher than those who went alone or with other female companions. Even those who brought their kids along recorded lower levels of stress than those accompanied by their husbands.

Women do have a greater affinity to what we think of as shopping—walking at a relaxed pace through stores, examining merchandise, comparing products and prices, interacting with sales staff, asking questions, trying things on, and ultimately making a purchase. Even when shopping for the mundane, everyday necessities, even when the shopping experience brings no particular pleasure, women tend to do it in a dependable, agreeable manner. Women take pride in their ability to shop prudently and well.

When a woman goes out shopping, she will buy something, usually for somebody else or 'for the house'. What makes women such heroic shoppers? The nature-over-nurture advocates make out that the prehistoric role of women as homebound gatherers of roots, nuts and berries, rather than roaming hunters of game proves a biological inclination towards skillful shopping.

And when women weren't working outside, shopping gave them a good excuse to sally forth, to get away from the monotony and cares of housekeeping. With women increasingly joining the workforce, shopping is no longer the great escape. Indeed it's now something that must be crammed into tight spaces between job and commuting and home life.

Still shopping seems unchanged as a social, recreational activity for women. They like to shop with friends, egging each other on and saving each other from ill-advised purchases (one can't imagine two men setting off on a day of hunting for the perfect bathing trunk). Studies show that when two women shop together, they often spend more time and money than women alone. They certainly out-shop and outspend women saddled with male companions, or even kids.

For many women there are psychological and emotional aspects of shopping that are just plain absent in men. Women tend to tally up coolly the pros and cons of every purchase. They can trudge from shop to shop looking for a bargain, placing little value on their time and energy. In fact they take pride in their ability to make the best possible purchase.

Possibly the ideal place to study female shopping behaviour is in front of the greeting cards rack. Women will devote quite a bit of time studying card after card—picking up, opening and reading—to find the one that speaks their hearts.

Shopping is actually exhausting work, but women are trained for it from infancy. Girls begin shopping before they have money to spend. Shopping often presented to women as recreation, and they fall for the cheat, cautions Germaine Greer.

Incidentally, any wife watching the family budget knows better than to send her husband to a shopping centre with kids. Men are particularly suggestible to the entreaties of children.

You see a man impatiently move through a store to the section he wants, pick something up, and then almost abruptly, he's ready to buy. Men often forget their collar or waist size. Try to imagine a woman who doesn't know her bra size. Impossible.

It's only at computer hardware and software purchasing that you see men spending time unhurriedly, or at music shops and stores dealing with car accessories.

The Deliverance of Divorce

In 'no-fault' divorce, none of the two parties is deemed either "guilty" or "innocent".

Initiated in the USA, the above position has now gained acceptance in the bulk of the Western world. Gone is the traditional concept where one party was held responsible for the marital break-up, and the courts determined who that was. In a manner, the whole moral framework of marriage, who-did-what-to-whom, lies abandoned. A unilateral assertion by one party that their marriage has 'irretrievably broken down' is deemed enough. This is a consequence of the new no-consent rule (something entirely different from the former mutual-consent provisions). The mandatory pre-divorce separation periods have also been largely done away with. The prevailing socio-psychological climate considers marriage as too complex a human relationship to lend itself to any accurate or worthwhile dissection by an outside agency.

The divorce proceedings, that way, have become almost no adversarial in nature and gender-neutral in character based only on the criterion of "irreconcilable differences". The marital property (acquired during that particular marriage phase) is divided equally unless—and that's the latest trend—the couple have already entered into a pre-nuptial arrangement on the subject. What remains for the judge is to award alimony, if any, mostly looking to her "need" and his "ability" to pay. If there are children, their custody is decided "in the best interests of the child".

Marriage as a social institution is many thousand years old but ideas on marriage and divorce have undergone dramatic changes in the last hundred years. During the preceding century, it was mainly moored to sexual morality, impotence or desertion of the husband, or adultery and loose-living of the wife dominated the divorce scene. The strong feminist movement advocating equality of sexes and greater freedom of female action, coupled with the coming of women into workforce in huge numbers, added new dimensions.

Half of today's marriages in the USA (the highest rate in any developed country) are expected to end in divorce. Yet it is confidently made out that the institution of marriage itself is not really threatened. It is something like the British proclaiming, "The King is dead. Long live the King." People mostly marry and often hurry to remarry; their expectations from marriage are high, perhaps unduly high.

With no party to blame, the judges are not inclined to award much alimony (which anyway is not easy to collect when awarded). Alimony grants are generally given for short periods; more to enable her to retrain herself for a living. Men and women being theoretically equal, she's supposed to get on her own at the earliest.

What sort of a deal does her Indian counterpart—the typical middle-class Hindu housewife—receive when her sacramental wedlock breaks down? She has often the option, contrary to what usually obtains in the West, to move back to her parents' home; in fact, she may have already done so when her marriage started coming under serious strain. The children, if any, staying with grandparents or near relatives undergo a lesser loss of affection and care. But there and then her advantages come to an abrupt end. The ignominy of a broken marriage is a continuing embarrassment to her parents, besides to herself (marriage breakdowns are usually blamed on women then men, more for the former's failure). If she strikes out on her own, and that also in the relative anonymity of an urban setting, her life as single, particularly if still young, is rarely free from unsolicited and harnessing male advances (mostly from men with no marriage on their minds), and the living dread of any aspersions getting cast on her character. It could well become an abyss of loneliness and despair. Economic hardships she surely suffers, but she is evidently more reconciled to want than slings and arrows of calumny.

Studies bring out that many Indian marriages virtually flounder in the early acclimatization phase; not infrequently within days of marriage. It is common to come across matrimonial advertisements saying "Divorcee after one month of marriage", or "Respectfully and legally divorced after few days of marriage". This is perhaps inevitable in the context of arranged marriages, and the majority of our marriages are parentally arranged.

Records of divorce proceedings substantiate the general impression that in most cases the gravamen is cruelty—actual physical cruelty like beating, confinement, deprivation of proper food and rest. Or, it can be obvious mental cruelty like abuses and taunts. Dowry dissatisfaction creates problems but its percentage in marriage-wrecking is yet not alarming (though marital disputes and discord from unsatisfied desires for customer goods are steadily on the increase). A sensitive wife may well conclude that she can't take it any more, and manages to move back to her parents or brothers. The marriage has evidently broken down.

But her troubles may be just beginning.

Divorce proceedings in our courts take on an average 3 to 4 years, sometimes 7 to 8. And this period of uncertainty, divorcees admit, is often mentally more taxing than the post-divorce. Leaving aside a mutual-consent application filed jointly, the proceedings take unduly long. Even uncontested cases, which constitute a majority, simply linger on.

The law wants the court to try its hand at reconciliation. Where the parties, their parents, relatives and friends have failed, what precisely can an impersonal, busy court do except some sermonizing? The problem may be too basic for a simplistic patch-up.

A stage has possibly reached when the whole matter would merit a re-look; the law needs to fall in line and facilitate the inevitable trend. High marital happiness does not necessarily reside within a rigid framework of marital indissolubility. Whether marriages of older days were actually happier may well nigh be a myth? Anyway, people—more so upwardly mobile younger women—want a higher emotional content in marriage, more of mutual respect than subjection, more of volition than direction.

No one imagines our going whole hog the Western way, but an easier and a quicker divorce can serve as an escape route, the ultimate weapon of deliverance, when a marriage turn "intolerable".

Remarriage is an option but not the solution. Divorced women marry less than divorced men, and again many Indian women remarry under pressure, more from pressures arising out of staying single. A more humane and self-respecting approach lies in their enhanced economic strength, buttressed with progressive divorce laws and a understanding social milieu.

Whether some people like it or not, it is certain that the incidence of divorce is to rise sharply in the coming years, and so the process needs to be made quicker and easiest. In line with modern trends, it is high time the country makes suitable legislation to give equitable rights to the divorced and separated.

Epilogue

How to be happily married? This is a million-dollar question. Marriage is such a unique equation between the partners, it hardly lends itself to any generalization. Yet a few words are ventured on the subject.

As mentioned in the prologue, what's crucial in a marriage is the presence of mutual respect between the partners; respect for each other's mental maturity, respect for each other's lifestyle, and mutual physical attraction, all this backed by a firm commitment to one's marriage partner. And the same can be carried through their middle age and even thereafter. Under such ideal conditions, a man married for thirty years was heard to remark, "The woman I love happens to be my wife."

A marriage is enlivened when a couple indulge in frequent touching and petting. The amount of kisses that they have in early years need not decline drastically in later years.

Added to this, a certain sense of humour helps—humour that can laugh off a minor irritation, and turns off a petty quarrel to a smile, or just shrugs it off. A partnership enlivened by a dash of light-heartedness on both sides can see this quality enrich a marriage.

Index

A

A Gourmet Guide to Love Making, 57
Accidental affairs, 67
Adolescent in family
  Impact of, 113-15
Adult children, 135
Adultery, 70
Advertising and consumerism, 84
Affluent oldsters, 175-78
  vs traditional oldies, 176
Ageing, 72
  and retirement, 172-73
  life satisfaction, 173
  morale, 172
Alex Comfort
  approach to sex, 57

B

Bathrooms (separate)
  and happy marriages, 182
Bellow Saul
  on mid-life years, 163-64
Birth control
  male vs females, 103
Birth order
  significance, 98
  theory, 99
Birthdays
  and anniversaries, 188
Budgerigar mothers, 113

C

Cancers in men/women, 140
Can't do's
  in marriage, 211-213
Cars /driving
  quarrels, 207-209
Child development, 116
Childless by choice, 88
Childlessness, 87
  handling, 89
Children
  as sex hazards, 64
China
  one child policy, 92
  son preference, 92
Chronic Fatigue Syndrome, 148
  causes, 148
Clutter
  coping with, 193-96
Communication
  in marriage, 180
Compatibility, 165
Compliment giving, 192
Compulsive Sexual Behaviour, 73
Consumerism, 83
Conversation with partner, 193
Cooling Effect, 61-62
Corporate wife, 33

role, 33
Counter productive discussions, 182
Cyber affairs, 71

D

Demant William
(sleep specialist), 109
Detective techniques
on cheating husbands, 71
Devalued dads, 118-20
Disengagement theory
in old, 173
Divorce
proceedings, 219, 221
options after, 220
Double bed dynamics, 185
Dr Joyce Brothers
on long lasting
sexual relationships, 144
Drinking
in women, 152
limits, 153-54
notions of, 151
problems, 150
Dual Career Couples
Sex life, 58-60
Dust mites, 155
habitat, 156-57

E

Earn and spend
syndrome, 82-84
Egg donors, 107
Eichel W Edward
study on simultaneous orgasm, 55
Elderly parent, 140
Employed vs
unemployed wives, 37
Employees obligations
at work, 25
Empty Nest syndrome, 132-35, 159
Equal Employment Opportunity Commission (US), 26
Equality for sex, 56
Eriksons secret
of happy marriage, 179
Excuses for sex, 56
Eyler and Baridin
on sexual etiquette at work, 20-21

F

Family meal, 123-26
Fatigue factors, 149
Female infanticide, 102
First born, 98
First time father
case, 100-101
Forgetful husbands, 201-202

G

Gender equation
changes, 215-16
Gift
giving - receiving, 189-90
Grandparents, 136
role, 137
status change, 138

H

Hacker, Andrew
Mismatch : The Growing Gulf Between Women and Men, 214
Happiness, 82
Happy marriage, 179
ways of, 179

do's and don'ts, 180
Harris, Judith Rich (author)
observations, 115-18
Health disorders
and sexual acxtivity, 171
Heart rate
in intercourse, 171
Hoffman Dr Ronald L.,
on fatigue factors, 149
Homely
meaning, 12
Honeymoon, 14
exotic locations, 15
planning, 15
food/ drinks, 16
Hostile work environment, 24
Human sexuality
studies, 170
Humour
in marrying, 179-80
Hunter and
gatherer approach, 79
Husbands neglecting health, 145
wifes predicament, 145
Husbands silence, 192
Hydraulic Pump Theory, 71

I

Incompatability, 165
India scene of
sexual harassment, 26
Infidelity, 67
in women-factors, 69
myths, 69-70
types, 67
Inhibited Sex Drive Syndrome, 53
IPC
on sexual harasment, 26
Irritating husbands, 206
IVF, 105

J

Joint Family Living, 134
Joy of Sex, 57

K

Kamasutra, 57

L

Last born, 98
Latecomers (childbirth), 94
cases, 94-95
categories, 95-96
Laura Kipnis
- From Against Love : a Polemic, 210
Listening husbands, 203-204
Live - In couples, 13
Long marriages
Sexual Liveliness, 61-62
Love marriage, 12
incidents, 13

M

Man-woman friendship
challenges, 23
myth, 22
Marital sex, 54
Marriage
changes in, 191
Maternal employment
effect, 36
Medicine taking, 146
suggestions, 147
Men
health problems, 143-44
immune system, 143
Men
relationship with body, 146

Middle - age
married life in, 159
mate handling, 160
patterns/categories, 161
sexual life, 160
Middle Class, 82
Middle years, 162
sexuality, 164
Mini Honeymoon, 16
Money
and happiness, 80-81
in marriage, 77
matters, 76
meaning, 75
Money Equation
Case history, 78-80
Mother/ daughter in law
Brazilian courses on, 129
changes in, 130
conflicts, 129-31
Multiple births
in IVF, 105

N

Nagging, 197
Non-sexual love, 20
Non-sexual touching, 191

O

Ogden Nash
words for husbands, 207
Older parents, 96-97
Only child/onlies, 90-93
achievements, 93
prejudice, 93
Optimum Age
at marriage, 12
Orgasm (women's), 55
Overseas honeymooning, 14

P

Parent - offspring conflict, 111-12
Parenting a parent
dilemmas of, 141
Parents role reversal, 140
Peers vs parents
in teenagers, 115
Philandering, 68
justification, 71
Physiological changes, 170
Picky eating, 126
Playing one parent
against the other, 110-11
Pornography, 64-66
Procreative/recreative sex, 169
Professionals
marriage between, 13
Put-0ffs, 61

R

Reference group theory, 174
Remarriage, 222
Requisites for a girl, 12
Reserved child, 117
Retirement
and married life, 166-67
and working wife, 168
Romantic infidelity, 68
Rosenblatl, Paul
on bed sharing, 185-87

S

Same/Rival company couples
coping strategies, 29
School timings
changes, 107
in US, 109
Sex addiction
controlling, 72

Sexual attraction
in co-workers, 20, 22
Sexual dysfunctions, 171
Sexual Harassment
agency monitoring, 26
at workplace, 23
Definition, 23
EEC, 25
forms, 24
India, 26
Insurance, 25
measures, 26
suits, 25
US scenario, 16
Sexual life in middle age couples, 160, 168
Sexy couples, 63
Shopping women vs men, 216-19
Sleep deprivation, 102
Social drinking, 153
Social Network sites, 13
Society standards
and sex activity, 171
Sperm banking, 106
Stop Fighting About Money, 77
Successful Husbands, 31-32
Successful wives, 29, 43-44
attitude to, 30
fear, 30-31]
threat of, 29-30
Sulking, 199

T

T.V ads
and children, 120-22
Teenage girl
parenting, 114
Teenagers
and sleep time pattern, 108, 110
sleepy, 108-109
Teenagers driving, 127-28
Television Hug, 66-67
Testosterone levels
impact of, 144
Testosterone/Progesterone levels, 60
The Adonis Complex, 145
The Art of Hugging, 66
The Birth Order Book, 99
The Nurture Assumption, 115
Tired All the Time, 149
Toman, Walter (Family Therapist), 99
Toxic pollutants, 155
vulnerable section, 155
breeding ground, 156
Tripping/ falling episodes
in old, 174-75
in young, 174-75
Tubectomy, 104
TV role
in consumerism, 84
Two income couples
money management strategies, 80
Two career marriages, 30

U

Understanding Prescription Drugs, 147
Untidyness
coping with, 196-97
Updike John
novels on
middle age vs younger marriage, 162-63

V

Vaccuum cleaning, 156

Vasectomy, 103
- vs Tubectomy, 103-104

W

Wifely likes / dislikes, 213
Wife's birthday, 187
Withdrawing
- from a vicious discussion, 181

Without Child, 88
Women
- sexual capacities, 169

Women drinkers, 153
- categories, 154

Working fathers, 37-38
- stress, 38

Working from home, 39-41
- perspective, 41

Working men/women
- differences in abilities, 49-51

Working mothers, 34
- daughters of, 46
- health, 34
- impact on
- on children, 36
- psychological health, 35
- recreation, 35

Working woman, 45
- home of, 47
- reasons to work, 45-46
- world of, 47

Workplace
- attraction, 20
- friendship, 19-21
- marriages within, 13, 19